Carolyn takes the r(
Street where love t
have called it home.

Pastor Rick Warren, Senior Pastor, Saddleback Church
Lake Forest, California

In this finely written memoir, Carolyn evokes the heart of our country, its green pastures and peonies, loving, bright, resourceful people who find joy in each other, their community, and the bounty of the land. *608 Randolph Street* is filled with humor and poetry, stories that bring a family and gifts of an earlier era alive.

Mary Jane Roberts, award-winning author, poet, playwright, and teacher
Malibu, California

One of the most beautiful and well-written books that I have read, funny, tearful, strengthening and historical. It brings back memories of the twentieth century in happenings so similar to any American small town, but so well depicted in Bedford, Iowa.

Audrey Comport, author, Fulbright Scholar, and member of the Advisory Panel for *British Heritage Magazine*
Waynesburg, Pennsylvania

Carolyn captures the essence of Midwest small town life, circa 1940s to 1960s, in the stories about her family and her town, which she recounts with warmth, tenderness, and humor. Its universal appeal will pull many readers into nostalgia for their own experiences.

Louise Novinger Merkle,
Elementary teacher
Oakland, Iowa

A wonderful, heart-warming journey with a Midwestern family, author Carolyn Cummings has done a remarkable work of telling her family story. She has definite skills describing her home, her hometown, and above all, her relationships with her family in a very creative, personal way. As I read *608 Randolph Street* I was there with her and her family. This book, definitely a labor of love on her part, will touch the hearts of all who travel with her, growing up in a small Iowa town.

Pastor Dick Krambeck
Atlantic, Iowa

608 Randolph Street

Bedford, Iowa

As I Remember It

Carolyn May Cummings

Copyright © 2008 by Carolyn May Cummings

All rights reserved. No part of this book shall be reproduced or transmitted in any form or by any means, electronic, mechanical, magnetic, photographic including photocopying, recording or by any information storage and retrieval system, without prior written permission of the publisher. No patent liability is assumed with respect to the use of the information contained herein. Although every precaution has been taken in the preparation of this book, the publisher and author assume no responsibility for errors or omissions. Neither is any liability assumed for damages resulting from the use of the information contained herein.

ISBN 0-7414-5008-9

Published by:

1094 New DeHaven Street, Suite 100
West Conshohocken, PA 19428-2713
Info@buybooksontheweb.com
www.buybooksontheweb.com
Toll-free (877) BUY BOOK
Local Phone (610) 941-9999
Fax (610) 941-9959

Printed in the United States of America
Published May 2009

Dedication

This collection of stories is dedicated to my sister and brother, Elaine and Jim, my co-authors. Your countless suggestions and generous help made them possible.

Norman Rockwell said, "The commonplaces of America are to me the richest subject in art;

> boys batting flies on vacant lots,
>
> little girls playing jacks on the front steps,
>
> old men plodding home at twilight, umbrellas in hand,
>
> the things we have seen all our lives, and overlooked."

Like Rockwell, I cherish the memories of everyday events when we were kids, before we realized how fortunate we were. Those make the richest subjects for stories;

> sitting on Daddy's knee
>
> singing around the piano
>
> catching lightning bugs at dusk,
>
> sitting around the dinner table together.

We were extremely fortunate and blessed to have wonderful parents, caring neighbors, and close connections with our large extended family.

As you can see by the photo, I got an early start on this book. I always thought that someday I would write stories about our family to pass on to our children and grandchildren.

Thank you for all your love and support.

Love,
Carolyn

CONTENTS

Foreword i
Thank You iii

Chapter One: Beginnings

The Old House Has a History 1
The Year Is 1938 8
The Year Is 1940 11
The Year Is 1948 14
Another Baby 16
Poem: The Peonies Bloomed in May 18

Chapter Two: Neighbors on Randolph Street

Our Neighbors on Randolph Street 19
Harmon and Bessie 22
Grandma and Grandpa Cummings 24
Ivan and Esta and Jeanne Wells 26
The Gamet Family 31
The Lewis Family 32
Jess and Ethel 34
Mrs. Johnson 38
Poem: Grandma's Gifts 42

Chapter Three: The Buildings at 608 Randolph Street

The Shed 45
The Chicken House 46
The One Car Garage 48
The Old Red Barn 49

The House 53
Poem: The Music of the Sunset 58

Chapter Four: Family History

The Courtship of Carl and Helen 61
Daddy's Parents... 65
Poem: Our Song 74
Mama's Parents 77
Where's Grandpa?... 86
Mother's Club Program... 88
Cousins... 95
Daddy's Guided Tour 101

Chapter Five: Early Memories

On Daddy's Knees 115
Bibbins Park 118
Mama Liked Curls... 120
Life Around the Piano 124
Music, Music and More Music 128
There Was a War Going On 131
Monday was Always "Warsh" Day............................ 137
"Tiny" and the Dry Cleaning Truck 143
Dear Santa 144
Summer Vacations 148
Baby Brother 155

Chapter Six: Animals and Pets

Reigning Cats and Dogs 159
Jimmie's Pet Calf 164

On Top of Ol' Smokey and Other Equines................166
Bounce and Lucy................172

Chapter Seven: Favorite Lines and Stories
Favorite Lines and Stories................175
More Favorite Lines and Stories................184

Chapter Eight: Growing Up In Bedford
A Lick and a Promise................191
Sunday School and Church................193
Number Please................199
Wheels................203
The Good Ol' Days................207
Mother's Accident................234
Radio and Television................237
Mother was a Quilter................241
The Fourth of July................245
Did Mama Ever Sit Down?................249
The *Bedford Times Press*................252
Poem: Billy Lambert................255

Chapter Nine: Siblings
My Brother, the Actor................257
My Sister, the Middle Child................263

Chapter Ten: Cherished Memories
Sunday Evening Telephone Chats................265
A Spark Rekindled................269

Found 271
Poem: I'm Home 274
Saying Goodbye 276

Appendices 281
Appendix 1
Newspaper Article by I.W. Scherich 281

Appendix 2
Alonzo Cummings 286

Appendix 3
The Rose Bush 292

Appendix 4
Revolutionary War Patriot 295

Appendix 5
Rev. Jesse Herbert 298

Foreword

Since the house at *608 Randolph Street* in Bedford, Iowa, was the only home to my sister, my brother, and me, and since most of these stories originated from there, *608 Randolph Street* seemed like the most appropriate title for this book. Randolph Street, the last street at the west edge of town, was a gravel road for much of the time that I lived there. Wild violets sprang up every spring in the ditches on both sides of the road.

This collection of short stories was written over a period of five years. Many were inspired in my writing class, some were written in the middle of the night when a story surfaced out of nowhere, and some were stories that my brother and sister and I recreated together as we remembered them.

Looking out the back door of our house, we could see our acreage with a pasture, a grape arbor, fruit trees, Mom's large garden, animals, a barn, and other small buildings. From the front door, we could see the grand old clock atop the ornate courthouse about half a mile to the east. Beyond the courthouse, we saw the rolling hills of southern Iowa east of our little town. The back door was in the country; the front door was in town.

Bedford is typical of hundreds of small towns in the heartland of America. While I was growing up Bedford had a population of about 2,000. On Main Street in the business area, the stores stayed open on Saturday night when the farmers came to town. That was typical of life in a small rural community. Life seemed less complicated then. Small town life in the 1940s and 50s had a special flavor that has been lost in modern society. I would like future generations to know about that time in America.

Our country was at war during many of those years, but we were united in the war effort. We worked hard, shared many of the same values, helped our neighbors, and grew up in close-knit families. Mine was a loving family where I found security, guidance, and good times. Sunday school and church filled our Sunday morning. Extended family gatherings were important. We made our own fun and entertainment. I learned the meaning of words like **sincere** and **honest** by observing people on Main Street, at church, at school, and at home.

There was nothing unusual or spectacular about Bedford, Iowa, or Randolph Street or the house at 608. However, it's the place I still call home.

These are my memories and stories about that place and time.

Thank You

To **Auntie Blanche,** for sharing your memories and supplying me with new information.

To **Jeanne and Ruth**, former Randolph Street neighbors, for answers to things I didn't know or had forgotten.

To **Mary Jane Roberts**, my first writing teacher, poet, author, playwright, and encourager. I always looked forward to getting up for your Monday morning writing class. Most of these stories were started there.

To **Kevin,** for your generosity and expertise in setting up my computer and printer in 2005. It was a turning point.

To **Joe,** for setting up my new computer in 2007 and your expert instruction. Your diehard persistence and patience has, indeed, earned you the title of ***Bulldog.***

To **Marie, Sandra, Celeste, Althea, and Jeannie,** for reading stories and offering suggestions.

To **Heidi**, for your help with copying and binding the first manuscript. Your offer to help came when I needed it most.

To **Kathleen**, fellow writer, friend, and computer wizard. Your help with the scanner and computer was invaluable.

To **Judy and Joan**, the *dynamic duo*. Your professional editing is appreciated more than you can imagine.

CHAPTER ONE

Beginnings

The Old House Has a History

The old house at *608 Randolph Street* in Bedford, Iowa, has a history, no doubt about that. It's been in our family since 1934. Shortly after Dad left this earth in May of 2003, my brother and sister and I started on the most daunting task I've ever experienced--scouring through shelves, closets, and boxes of treasures in the old house.

New surprises greeted us every day. We would be in various locations of the house, upstairs or down, each exploring a corner, when one of us would break the silence with, "Wow, guess what I just found!" or "You'll just never believe this!" Several days of this routine, in the weeks that followed Dad's death, brought back loving reminders of things we had almost forgotten. Mom and Dad had preserved memories for us, and I felt the need to write about them.

Carl and Helen Cummings, my dad and mom, were savers. They knew they were. They didn't even try to throw things away. Their memories of the Great Depression years were responsible for that. Several times Daddy lamented, "Oh my, you kids are going to have a big job, someday." He was right. The forgotten keepsakes brought back pieces of our past, a collection of memories that we decided must be preserved for our children.

Writing and recording these stories is the second most daunting task I've ever undertaken.

Perhaps the best place to begin is with the house itself, the dwelling at *608 Randolph Street*. Among the treasures we found in the house was a copy of an Enid,

Oklahoma, newspaper clipping, probably written around the turn of the twentieth century. I.W. Scherich, a Civil War veteran from Pennsylvania, built the house. The article gives his first-hand account of his experiences in the war and his meetings with President Lincoln.

A complete text of the article is in Appendix 1.

The headline in the Enid newspaper reads as follows:

Enid Soldier Relates Days With Lincoln

I.W. Scherich, 823 West Randolph,

Saw Famous President Five Times

Speaks Kindly of Words of Leader

"Emancipator" Honored on Each Side of Mason-Dixon Line

Here is a summary of the article:

Mr. Scherich enlisted in Company "A" of the Eighteenth Pennsylvania Cavalry in 1862 and was assigned to defend Washington D.C. He told of the visits from the President and his habit of leaving his carriage and walking among the soldiers. After defending Washington, Mr. Scherich's division quickly found themselves in action at Gettysburg. Many of the men from the Eighteenth died there in those four well-documented days in July. From there they saw many heartbreaking campaigns along the Richmond-Washington Road. In the Shenandoah Valley, Mr. Scherich lost an arm. After many weeks in a Philadelphia hospital, he returned to his home in the Pennsylvania hills. The news, that the war was over traveled slowly. Rejoicing was short lived. On April 15, 1865, word traveled like wildfire across the country by word of mouth that President Lincoln had been assassinated. Mr. Scherich wrote the article some sixty-two years after the events he described, but he could never forget the serious and kind face of the President.

Attached to the newspaper copy was an additional page that was added by my father, Carl Cummings. Daddy liked to document things. In the familiar type of his favorite old Underwood manual typewriter - a gift from my mother in 1934 - he added this additional page of information.

Some of the following information was obtained from Clyde E. Scherich, who was the son of the builder, I.W. Scherich. These paragraphs are reproduced exactly as Daddy wrote them:

Clyde E. Scherich said that Alva and Bill Baldwin of Pennsylvania and West Virginia came with his father, I.W. Scherich, to Bedford, Iowa, and built the house at 608 Randolph Street in 1875.

The building materials were brought up from St. Joseph, Missouri, about seventy miles south of Bedford, and after the house was built in Bedford, the two brothers moved to St. Joseph, where they lived and built houses as long as they were able. The house at 608 Randolph Street is the only house that they built in Bedford.

The tulip tree and the chestnut tree were brought from the old Scherich farm, located part in West Virginia and part in Pennsylvania. The trees were balled and burlaped and he brought them to Iowa with him on the train and set them out in the front yard at 608 Randolph Street.

The tulip tree lived and bloomed each season around Memorial Day and it died in the summer of 1972. It was removed in September of 1972 being ninety-seven years old at that time. The chestnut tree is now in its third generation from the original tree as it sprouts from the roots. The nuts do not mature since it is the only chestnut tree here and does not pollinate.

I.W. Scherich died on October 26, 1928.

With a sense of wonder I think of this determined war hero coming west, bringing two friends, perhaps with families. Before the town of Bedford was much more than a few stores, livery stables, harness shops, houses, and mud roads, he selected the spot on the hill where he wanted his house. Founded in 1853, Bedford was still a young community.

Clyde E. Scherich was born in the house at 608 Randolph Street. After his family moved, the Donaldson family bought the house. The Donaldsons were the parents of Opal Ahrens (of Ahrens Drug store). It was Opal's mother who approached my parents, newly-weds in 1934, to offer them the house. My parents moved into 608 Randolph Street in October 1934.

However, this was not the first time that my Dad was at home on Randolph Street. My paternal grandparents, Clyde and Florence Cummings, along with Daddy and his sister, Blanche, had lived at 704 Randolph Street, which is one house north of 608. In 1928 they moved there from a house on Jackson Street in Bedford.

Dad lived with his parents at 704 Randolph until he married Mom. He told me once that his parents "commenced to wonder" if he was ever going to get married.

Photograph of Carl and dog, Buddy, taken in front of 704 Randolph Street in the mid-1930s

Dad was not quite twenty-seven years old when he married Mom. Their immediate honeymoon nest was a house on Court Street. In October 1934, the house at 608 Randolph Street became their home together and remained so for the next sixty-five years.

Photograph of Blanche Cummings with neighbor, Jeanne Wells, and dog, Buddy. Mid 1930s

Aunt Blanche, who is eight years younger than Dad, remembers the house at 704 Randolph as her home from the time she was twelve years old until she was twenty. There are lots of memories on the hill for her.

The houses on the west side of Randolph Street were built at the crest of a hill with several acres of pasture to the west. The land dipped into a creek at the lowest elevation. The generous, sloping front yards are about an acre in size, a fact that is not easily forgotten by those of us who propelled a manual lawn mower (the "puff and grunt" type) over the front lawns.

My Grandpa Clyde passed away on June 2, 1960, in the house at 704 Randolph Street. Grandma Florence continued to live there until her death on July 5, 1970. After that Mom and Dad remodeled the house and kept it as a rental for a few years.

In 1974, my brother Jim, his wife Rosalyn, and their baby daughter Carla, moved back to Bedford and took over Dr. Don Anderson's Veterinary business. Jim bought his Grandpa's house at 704 Randolph Street, becoming the third generation to buy up on the hill.

When Daddy died, the house at 608 Randolph Street was empty for the first time in sixty-nine years. The future of the old house and property was uncertain for a while. Then, quite by surprise, Jim's son Jeff and his wife Tara decided that they would like to buy Grandpa Carl's house. Like father, like son.

So in August, 2003, the fourth generation of our family bought a home on Randolph Street.

Clyde…Carl…James…Jeffrey

Carl was the only son of Clyde and Florence.

James is the only son of Carl and Helen.

Jeff is the only son of Jim and Rosalyn.

This appeals to my sense of order, but it doesn't end there.

On June 10, 2004, almost a year after Dad's death, his little namesake, Tristen Carl Cummings, was born. The first son of Jeff and Tara, he is the first child in the fifth generation of our family to live on the Randolph Street properties.

Okay, little Tristen, it's your turn.

The house at 608 Randolph Street today with new owners, Jeff and Tara Cummings

The Year Is 1938

In 1938 swing was popular, as Benny Goodman, The King of Swing, delighted audiences at Carnegie Hall. His all-star band consisted of Harry James, Ziggy Elman, Lionel Hampton, Gene Krupa and Teddy Wilson. Benny hired the best musicians for his band, regardless of color.

Artie Shaw recorded the Cole Porter tune, "Begin the Beguine," and sold more than a million 78 rpm records.

Glen Miller, born in neighboring Clarinda, Iowa, discovered his unique big band sound, heavy on the saxophone.

Irving Berlin's 1918 tune was sung by Kate Smith for the first time. The name of the tune: "God Bless America." Both tune and singer gained popularity.

Snow White and the Seven Dwarfs, Disney's first feature-length cartoon film, sent his reputation soaring. Jimmy Stewart starred in Frank Capra's *You Can't Take It with You*. Bette Davis and Henry Fonda made *Jezebel* a success. Spencer Tracy, Mickey Rooney, Katharine Hepburn, Cary Grant and Errol Flynn all had hits in Hollywood, California, that year. And 1938 was the year that Bob Hope first sang "Thanks for the Memory."

On October 30th, a young man named Orson Welles broadcast a Halloween scare on CBS. It was Howard Koch's version of H.G. Wells' novel: *War of the Worlds*. Over a million listeners panicked. Orson said he just intended to entertain. I was only two months old. I slept through the entire broadcast.

The number one comic strip character was a figure in blue and red tights, sporting a large **S** on his chest.

Thornton Wilder published *Our Town* in New York City, and Pearl S. Buck received the Nobel Prize for literature.

The Jefferson head nickel came into circulation. The DuPont Company in Delaware made the first nylon products as well as two other new products, Teflon and Fiberglass.

On July 3rd, President Franklin D. Roosevelt dedicated a monument at Gettysburg, marking that battle's 75th anniversary.

In October, the New York Yankees defeated the Chicago Cubs in the World Series, and in December, the National Football League championship was won by the Giants who defeated the Green Bay Packers.

"Wrong Way" Corrigan landed in Ireland instead of California!

The leaders of Great Britain, France, Italy, and Germany met in Munich in September hoping to end rumors of war in Europe. Japan shut the door on the Open Door Policy with the United States.

To start a car you needed to turn a key as well as push on a starter button located on the metal dashboard. The Packard was the car for those who could afford it, although Fords and Chevrolets were the favorites of middle class Americans.

The penny postcard had its green stamp imprinted in the corner and a three cent stamp would mail a first-class letter.

A little racehorse named Seabiscuit would not give up. He was the most written about public figure by newspaper columnists in 1938. Roosevelt was second. Hitler was third.

Some pretty significant events happened in 1938. On the 29th of August, I was born. I think 1938 was a good year.

I'm almost one year old in this picture with my parents.

The house in the background belongs to our neighbors, Harmon and Bessie.

The Year Is 1940

On November 2, 1940, when I was two years and two months old, my parents told me I had a baby sister. They named her Elaine Ann, without even consulting me!

Jukeboxes were popular in 1940, and for a nickel you could hear the hep sounds of Goodman and Dorsey, and everyone was doing the Lindy Hop.

Henry Fonda gained more fame in the new film, *The Grapes of Wrath*. Disney's animation produced *Fantasia*. CBS demonstrated a new technology in its infancy: color television. The average American home did not yet have black and white television.

Hemingway's new novel, *For Whom the Bell Tolls* brought him success, and as a war correspondent, he also covered the Japanese invasion of China.

Pulitzer Prizes were awarded to John Steinbeck for *The Grapes of Wrath*, and to Carl Sandburg for *Abraham Lincoln: The War Years*. Thomas Wolfe's book, *You Can't Go Home Again*, was published posthumously.

Hollywood awarded its first Oscar to a black actress, Hattie McDaniel, for her supporting actress role in *Gone with the Wind*, which was a hit the previous year. Also in Hollywood, Warner Brothers Studio introduced a new cartoon character, Bugs Bunny!

Social Security checks were received by the first recipients. Ida Fuller of Vermont received check #000-00-001 for the fair amount of $22.54.

President Roosevelt was called a warmonger by the country's isolationists, as he promised destroyers to Winston Churchill in an effort to help protect Britain against German U Boat attacks.

The nation's first peacetime military draft began in October.

Three days after my sister Elaine was born, President Roosevelt won a victory in the November 5th election, becoming the first president elected to a third term. My mother probably didn't vote that year.

American volunteer fighter pilots formed the Eagle Squadron in the R.A.F. in Great Britain and the U.S. managed to stay out of World War II for another year.

Further recovery from the depression years gave people more financial security.

The World Series was won by the Reds who defeated the Detroit Tigers. In the NFL, the Chicago Bears defeated the Washington Redskins by a record 73-0.

The Willy Jeep was introduced in 1940. That four wheel drive vehicle had a top speed of sixty-five miles an hour.

The 1940 census informed us that the population of the United States was 131.6 million and the average life expectancy was an astounding sixty-three years.

I was excited about having a baby sister.

1940 was a very good year!

*First photograph with baby sister Elaine.
She's the one that is fussing, and I don't look too happy.*

Baby sister Elaine with Mom and me

The Year Is 1948

In the ten years prior to 1948, the United States and the world had experienced extraordinary changes.

World War II had ended and recovery had begun all over the world. The first Baby Boomers were born, and for the next 14 years that population explosion made and changed history. Seventy-eight million Baby Boomers! That's a lot of babies, and my baby brother was one of them.

I remember the exact place where I was standing when Mom told Elaine and me that we were going to have a baby brother or sister. We had wanted one for several years. A baby was at the top of our wish list to Santa.

Baby James Carl Cummings was born on the 14th of January, 1948. Elaine was seven. I was nine years old.

In a departure from the car-side service, McDonald's opened a hamburger drive-up in San Bernardino, California. There were no car hops. The posted sign read: "Buy'em by the Bag." A hamburger cost fifteen cents, French fries were a dime, and milk shakes were twenty-five cents.

In August of that year, the United States came home from the Olympics in London with thirty-eight gold medals.

In November, Harry S. Truman won the presidential election in one of the big political upsets in American history.

Polaroid cameras made their debut, and television was becoming a permanent part of every American's life. Shows that had their start in 1948 were: *Candid Camera, The Milton Berle Show, Toast of the Town, Arthur Godfrey's Talent Scouts, Philco Television Playhouse,* and *Studio One.*

A tiny transistor revolutionized electronics.

Baseball's greatest slugger, Babe Ruth, died of cancer.

Eleanor Roosevelt's untiring efforts helped to pass the United Nations Declaration of Human Rights.

The Supreme Court declared prayer in schools was a violation of the Constitution. The United States recognized the new State of Israel on May 14, 1948.

Jockey Eddie Arcaro rode a young colt, Citation, to win the Triple Crown.

For many reasons 1948 was quite a year! Mom and Dad were ecstatic. They finally had a baby boy. Elaine and I finally had a baby brother. 1948 was a very, very good year.

Jimmie, age one, with Grandpa Clyde

Another Baby

I always thought that I was the oldest child in my family until the day when my parents explained that I was not their first child.

It happened on Memorial Day. The folks back home in Iowa call it Decoration Day. We were driving to the cemetery. I was in my usual place nestled between Mama and Daddy in the front seat of the old black '39 Ford. Three year old Elaine occupied Mama's lap.

As we drove into the cemetery entrance, my five year old curiosity prompted the question, "Who do we know here?"

Mama and Daddy spoke almost in unison. "I've been waiting for you to ask that."

That was the day I was told that a year before I was born, they had a baby boy. He was their first child, born on Father's Day. Baby Richard lived only three days. I remember looking at the little headstone differently that day. I had never been able to read it before. I wasn't sure how to react to this new set of feelings. They weighed heavily on my five-year-old heart. Mama's tears were unsettling. Daddy was very quiet.

Many of my questions about Baby Richard have remained unanswered. Relatives have filled me in on some details; others were discovered as my sister and I went through boxes of treasures in our parents' empty house. Baby Richard was born at home, but was taken to the hospital in St. Joseph, Missouri, on the third day. Dr. Hardin accompanied Daddy during that trip. Baby Richard died just as Daddy and Dr. Hardin were arriving at the emergency room. Both of my grandmothers stayed with Mama when her baby was taken away. I don't know if she ever saw her first-born child again. Daddy went to the funeral alone, since

Mama had had a tough delivery, and new mothers had to stay in bed for a week. Our family didn't have a family plot at the cemetery until that time. Then it became necessary.

Still trying to find some sense of closure to the death of baby Richard, Mama cried at the mention of it even fifty years later. Grandma Florence would also cry when she talked about that painful experience.

I resolved that the hurt in my parents' hearts would never go away. How their relationship with each other was scarred by that one sad event was something I could not change. I had to allow their quiet agony to remain inside their hearts, seldom asking questions.

In spite of the unanswered questions, there was one that we never had to ask. We never questioned our parents' love for us. I think that is, after all, the best legacy parents can leave their children.

The Peonies Bloomed in May

The peonies bloomed in May.
We'd await their arrival each spring.
The fragile pinks and reds
created rich mounds of color
along the sidewalk by our house.
Dew-laden in the morning,
their scent gave an innocent
sweetness to the air.

The peonies bloomed in May.
Small cemeteries across the prairie
burst into vivid color
as relatives remembered
their families and friends
by placing peonies on the headstones
at Graceland, Fairview, Old Memory,
and Hopkins on Memorial Day.

The peonies bloomed in May.
Few other perennials
blossomed in time for Memorial Day.
Mother's face was wet with tears
as bundles of peonies
were softly arranged over the markers
of her mother and father
and three-day-old baby boy.

The peonies still bloom in May
in a part of our land
that survived another winter
and gladly invites the springtime,
when crocus and daffodils and tulips
push their way through soft soil
announcing the proper time to welcome
the peonies in May.

CHAPTER TWO

Our Neighbors on Randolph Street

This stretch of road, about two blocks long, was our playground.

There was no need for a fence around the playground for protection. Our neighbors provided that. Like the old African proverb, "It takes a village to raise a child," the neighbors on Randolph Street helped to raise Elaine and Jim and me, as well as all the other kids who grew up there.

From Main Street at the south end of Randolph Street, to Polk Street at the north end, North Randolph Street was our extended yard and the neighbors were our extended family. It was safe and quiet like a sheltered cocoon.

The families all shared in both the good and bad seasons of each other's lives. We looked out for each other.

Only six houses occupied this stretch of road. These are the neighbors that lived on Randolph Street during the years I lived there, 1938-1960.

There were only four houses on the west side of North Randolph Street. From south to north these were the families:

Harmon and Bessie Miller and son Bobby

Our house was next.

Grandpa and Grandma Cummings

Ivan and Esta Wells and daughter Jeanne

The entire time I lived at *608 Randolph Street*, there was only one house on the west side that had a change of residents. That was Ivan and Esta Wells property at the north end. How's that for a stable neighborhood?

When Ivan was elected to the office of Taylor County Sheriff for two different terms, their family moved to the Sheriff's red brick house in the court yard downtown. When Ivan and Esta were not living on Randolph Street, Mr. and Mrs. Judd Caskey occupied their house. After the Wells sold their home, two other families lived in the house: the Ross Gamet family and the Bill Lewis family.

Our yards, both front and back, blended together. Fences were necessary in the pastures only for protection of our cattle and horses.

There were only two houses on the east side of Randolph Street. Directly across the street from our house was the home of Mrs. Johnson and her family. And Jess and Ethel Derrickson lived directly across the road from Ivan and Esta.

House numbers weren't important to anyone in town. We knew where everyone lived. If a visitor to Bedford needed directions to someone's home, any of our friendly gas station attendants could be of help.

The following pages contain some of the memories I have of each of these families, as I remember them.

Cousins, neighbors, and friends help celebrate my first birthday in the photograph taken in our front yard. Mrs. Johnson's house is in the background.

Left to right: back row: Johnny Novinger, Louise Novinger

Middle row, left to right: Bobby Miller, Helen Novinger Jeanne Wells, Ruth and Katherine Johnson

Babies in front: Mike Travis, Carolyn, Billy Rankin, and Cheryl O'Dell

Harmon and Bessie

Harmon and Bessie Miller had a big two-story house with lots of space for a family of three. Bob, their only child, was much older than me, but he came to my first birthday party. He probably could have found a more exciting way to spend a summer day, but he was there. Just proves to me that Randolph Street neighbors really were like an extended family.

Harmon was a tall, thin man who wore a serious expression on his face most of the time. He had a repair shop at the bottom of their hill. The little shop burrowed itself back into the steep bank that defined their side yard on Main Street. Harmon could repair anything. He reasoned that "If someone made it, I can fix it." From small appliances to tricycles, bicycles, wagons, and cars, Harmon could weld together anything that was broken.

On hot summer days, Elaine and I liked to set up a lemonade or Kool-Aid stand under the chestnut tree in the corner of our front yard. I guess we thought people would flock from town to our front yard and buy a cool drink. Cars didn't stop to buy; people didn't flock from town; nobody bought our lemonade or Kool-Aid except Harmon. We could always count on Harmon for a sale. Elaine remembers that we drank most of the Kool-Aid ourselves, which usually made us sick.

Bessie wore a hair net and an ankle-length dress most of the time. At the Cudahy plant, she candled eggs as they came along the conveyor belt.

Just west of the Miller's back door a real cave was nestled into the ground. We knew it was the safest place to wait out a tornado; much safer than the basements at our house or Grandma's house. Thankfully, we never had to run to the cave for protection.

Bessie and Harmon were proud of their son, Bob. He married Madge, had two children, Gary and Susie, and held a responsible position with Montgomery Ward in Kansas City, Missouri. They still sent Christmas cards to Daddy, as long as he lived at *608 Randolph Street*.

Harmon passed away first. Bessie lived in the big house alone, long after she retired from Cudahy's. Every morning when she got up, she raised the window shade in a north window of her house. That was her signal to Mom and Daddy that she was awake and fine. Long before medical alert systems, Bessie and my parents had worked out their own system. They took care of one another.

Bessie moved closer to her son in her later years and eventually, the old house stood empty. Windows were broken out and wild creatures lived inside. After the old house was gone a new manufactured house took its place.

Harmon's little repair shop has been gone a long time. There is no clue that his thriving business once stood at the corner. But the memories haven't gone away. Long time neighbors are like family.

Grandma and Grandpa Cummings

One house north of ours was the home of my paternal grandparents, Clyde and Florence Cummings. Daddy lived at this address until he married Mom in July of 1934.

A walk across the yard to Grandma's back door was made at least once daily by someone. As a little kid, I felt just as much at home at Grandma's as in my own house. The doors were never locked.

From our kitchen window we had a clear view of both the back and front porches, so we could keep up on the activities of Grandma and Grandpa. We could see Grandpa, in his bib overalls, carrying his milk bucket to the red barn to do the daily chores. We could see Grandma sitting in her swing on the front porch or working in her garden. Grandma came across the yard to our house everyday to catch up on the news. Grandpa came over every evening after supper to pick up the daily newspaper.

As a child, I didn't realize what an impact my grandparents would have on my life. They gave our lives more stability, showered us with compliments, and reassured us that we were the luckiest little kids that ever lived to have the best mom and dad in the world. All of these are ingredients for a happy childhood.

Ivan and Esta and Jeanne Wells

The Wells lived one house north of Grandpa and Grandma. Ivan was in the auctioneer business with my grandpa for almost forty years. He also was the Taylor County Sheriff from time to time.

Esta baked wonderful chocolate cakes. They made my mouth water as I sat in her kitchen and watched her layer the creamy fudge frosting over the top of the cake. Wondering if I would get a piece of her cake, I asked, "Are you gonna' take it to the chuch?" (That was my way of pronouncing the word church.) My question was answered when she cut the cake immediately and gave me a generous serving. I can still remember tasting that rich chocolate treat. Esta told my mother about this incident, and my mother loved to repeat it. This happened before my little sister was old enough to explore the neighborhood with me. I was probably about three or four years old.

Ivan and Esta's house had a real basement and a split level entrance on the south side. There was a cave in their back yard. Their house sat on a piece of property much like our acreage, with a barn and pasture to the west.

My dad's nickname for their daughter, Jeanne, was Skipper. She told me that Dad called her by that name for many years. Jeanne is about ten years older than I am.

Grandma Florence told me one day that Jeanne had lost an older sister. Eula died from lockjaw at the age of five. Jeanne was only three when she lost her sister, but even then she knew that things were not right. Recently, she told me that her parents never talked about Eula's death. Just like my parents when they lost baby Richard.

Ivan, Jeanne, and Esta on the porch of their original house before their new home was built.

One summer day when I was almost ten, Jeanne invited Elaine and me to participate in her wedding. She asked me to be her flower girl. Elaine was asked to be one of the ring bearers. Elaine's classmate and cousin of the groom, Harold Park, was the other ring bearer. Mom seemed pleased and excited to make our organdy dresses. Mine was pale pink. Elaine's was white. Harold wore a little white suit.

Our dresses had ruffles around the neckline, over the shoulders, and at the hemline. A sash tied in the back in a crisp, starched bow. Each dress had a long matching slip. Mom did a professional job as our seamstress. My little pink organdy dress still hangs in a closet in my home today.

The wedding took place on Sunday afternoon, August 22, 1948, at the Baptist Church on Main Street. It was an *extremely* hot day. The church had no air conditioning. Even the pastor shed his suit coat after the ceremony.

Bridesmaids, from left: Norma Park, Doris Andrew, Lorraine Rounds, Beverly Crawford, Bride: Jeanne Wells, Groom: Bob Park, Paul Wogan, Jack Gold, George O'Dougherty

Front row from left: Elaine Cummings, Harold Park, Carolyn Cummings

    Jeanne was a beautiful bride. I get choked up when I see a bride walking down the aisle with her father. I did that day, too. I was given a graceful straw basket decorated with pink ribbons. Inside were real rose petals. I got to walk down the aisle just ahead of the bride. I was a bit nervous when I dropped the petals along the aisle. I was concerned that the end of the petals might come before the end of the aisle.

    Fifty-five years later, at Jeff and Tara's wedding, I watched my three- year-old granddaughter, Zoe, drop petals on the same aisle in the same church. I was privileged to make her dress for the wedding. She wore the same gold locket I wore when I was flower girl for Jeanne and Bob's wedding. She took her job very seriously, practicing her 'aisling' (that's her word) along the sidewalk at Dad's house. For practice petals she picked dandelions from the yard and filled her basket with the yellow weeds. She made an adorable flower girl. Fortunately, by that time, the Baptist church was air-conditioned!

Jeanne and Bob eventually moved to Southern California and raised three children. Sometimes our summer trips from California to Iowa to see our parents and grandparents would coincide with theirs. When they traveled to Bedford, they always remembered to include a visit to Mom and Dad's house. I kept in touch with Ivan and Esta in Bedford after they moved to another address in Bedford.

Jeanne and Bob's daughter, Beth, was married in Santa Ana, California, on Jeanne and Bob's 40th anniversary. It was an occasion to get the original wedding party together. I was honored to be invited and to attend. Full circle. The wedding party hadn't changed one bit!

Now in retirement, both Jeanne and I can get together for brunch or lunch since we live in neighboring communities in South Orange County, California. We never run out of topics of conversation.

Our Dads shared the same birthday, July 31st

We knew many of the same people that lived in Bedford five decades ago.

We know many of the same people that live in Bedford today.

The auctioneer cry is close to our hearts.

We both grew up in Bedford, Iowa, and graduated from Bedford High School.

And we both lived on Randolph Street.

I'm so glad that we are neighbors once again.

Bob and Jeanne Park. Tustin, California. 2006

The Gamet Family

Ross and Velma Gamet became our new neighbors after Ivan and Esta Wells moved to another home in Bedford.

What a good-looking couple they were. And so were their children. Steve was the oldest. He was several years older than my little brother Jimmie. Dickie was the same age as Jimmie. Their third child, Jannie, was born in the house on Randolph Street. Elaine and I loved to baby sit with Jannie.

Ross was the manager of the new Hy-Vee grocery store on Madison. It was located at the corner of Jefferson, across from the Bedford Library. He had a good voice that was a welcome addition to the Presbyterian Church choir.

One day Dickie showed us his new puppy, Susie. The three of us kids had wanted a puppy for a long time. When we learned that Susie had a brother, the only one left in the litter, we began to put the pressure on Daddy and Mom to get a puppy for us.

After a few years as our neighbors, the Gamet family, moved to Loveland, Colorado.

When I graduated from college and began my teaching career in Denver, Colorado, I visited the Gamet family in nearby Loveland. It was good to see our former neighbors again and remember some of the good times we had together on Randolph Street.

The Lewis Family

William and Evelyn Lewis became our new neighbors after the Gamet family moved to Colorado. Everyone called them Bill and Evie. They had two children; Bill, Jr. and Patty. Patty was the same age as my little brother Jimmie. Always protected by Patty's little black dog, Bimmy, and Jimmie's little white terrier, Tippy, the two little kids played together every day.

William and Evie renovated their garage into a potato chip factory, a business they had before their move to Bedford. The fixtures were potato peelers and slicers, and a frying tub at the end of a conveyor belt where thin slices of potatoes dropped into the *hot* oil. William stood on a stool, with a long-handled wooden spoon in his hand and separated and moved the potatoes from the hot oil onto the exit belt. He wore a large white chef's apron and hat. This little converted garage was the setting of my first real job.

Working on a long metal counter, Verna Cox and I sorted and discarded any chips that weren't perfect. Bill was very particular about his quality control. After the sorting, the chips were scooped up into bags, weighed, and stapled. The bags were then boxed, ready for Bill to load into his panel truck for delivery to grocery stores the next day. Printed in bright blue letters on the bag was the name of the best potato chips anywhere: **Bill's Superior Chips.**

Bill and Evie were obviously very much in love. Bill would sing Evie's favorite song, "Tenderly," while he stirred the potatoes. Their romantic relationship was fascinating to me, especially since I was turning sweet sixteen that summer and had just fallen in love for the first time.

One of the benefits of my job was a big round tin can of fresh, hot potato chips to take home to my family. Evie made sure I never went home empty-handed. Another benefit of my first job was the short distance from home, made even shorter by walking through my grandparents' back yard.

The tub of sizzling hot oil sometimes heated the room temperature to 110 degrees in the garage-converted-factory. Yet I loved the experience of going to work and earning the amazing amount of fifty cents an hour!

The Lewis family came into our lives for a season and left us with fond memories. I still sort out the imperfect potato chips when a new bag is opened.

Jess and Ethel

Ethel would sit on her south porch in that favorite old rocker and wait and watch for Jesses' car to turn the corner at Main and Randolph Street. Jess and Ethel Derrickson lived across the street from Ivan and Esta's house. Our own endearing name for Mrs. Derrickson was Derrecky.

Jess worked at the Cudahy Plant. After work he'd stop at the Candy Kitchen to have a beer with his friends. Then he'd drive west to the top of Main Street, turn right onto Randolph and go to the second house on the right where Derrecky waited.

Elaine and I loved to visit Derrecky. We'd go over to her house and call through the screen door.

"Hello. Anybody home?"

Sometimes she'd say, "No," followed by her jolly laugh that rolled out of her and kept right on going. We loved to surprise Derrecky.

Elaine and I would sing duets, tell her riddles, make up stories, and roll down their steep bank by the porch. This was the same steep bank that they had to navigate every time they went to the outhouse. Quite a difficult trip for older folks, but we never heard them complain. Elaine and I didn't give much thought to the fact that Derrecky's house had no indoor plumbing, or for that matter, no running water in the kitchen. The pump beside the back porch brought them water for drinking, cooking, and bathing. That was just the way that Derrecky's house was.

I never heard her complain. Her slower, uncomplicated life style seemed to fit her. She always seemed genuinely happy. She always had time for two little girls who would wander over across the street and just love to be the center of her attention.

One of the duets that we sang was "Whispering Hope." I sang the soprano and Elaine sang the wordy alto part that seemed like two songs were going on at the same time. She requested that song more than any other.

The years went quickly by. Elaine and I outgrew the long, lazy summer evening visits on Derrecky's porch as we became busy with high school friends, and activities. Our visits were infrequent. She probably chuckled as she watched us learn to drive the family car down our steep driveway. I'm sure she saw us come and go with friends and with dates. Through our neighborhood network, mainly Grandma Florence, we never lost touch with the families on our street.

Then one day the Baptist pastor, Rev. Fred Cowles, called to say that Jess was dying and Ethel requested a visit from Carolyn and Elaine. They had moved to another house in Bedford by that time, a more modern house, as I remember.

There, we saw Derrecky being strong and loving as she cared for Jess. She asked him if he remembered the Cummings girls. He nodded. Derrecky said, "Sure he remembers you, sure he does" as she did the talking for her husband.

A few days later we got the call. Jess had died. Derrecky, our long time neighbor and friend, wanted Elaine and me to sing at Jess's funeral. She requested the song she had heard us sing many times, "Whispering Hope." By this time our voices had changed. I sang the wordy alto part and Elaine had developed a beautiful soprano voice. We felt privileged to sing for her and her family. I'd never thought of our song as a funeral number, but Derrecky caught a glimpse of hope in the message.

"Soft as the voice of an angel, breathing a lesson unheard.

Hope, with a gentle persuasion, whispers a comforting word.

Wait til the darkness is over, wait til the tempest is gone.

Hope for the sunshine tomorrow, after the shower is gone.

Chorus:

Whispering Hope, whispering hope,

Oh how welcome, how welcome the voice.

Making my heart, making my heart, in its sorrow,

Rejoice."

Reverend Fred Cowles, the Baptist pastor, told me before the service that it was always an easier task to preach a funeral if the deceased had accepted Jesus as his Savior. Jess had done that shortly before he died.

Derrecky went to live with her only child, a son and his wife, in another state after Jess died. I wish we'd had the time to visit with Derrecky more often before she left our town. But at the time I still didn't realize the gentle, yet profound, lessons I had learned from her. It's the same lesson that the Apostle Paul tells the Philippians in chapter 4, verses 11 and 12 of my favorite New Testament book:

"...for I have learned to be content whatever the circumstances.

I know what it is to be in need,

And I know what it is to have plenty.

I have learned the secret of being content in any and every situation..."

It was sometime later, when Elaine and I were in our twenties, that we learned that our former neighbor and friend, who sat in the rocker on her porch, had gone to her glory. I was thankful that she had shared a chapter in my childhood and showed me qualities of patience, kindness, contentment, love, joy and, always, hope.

Someone whom I least expected to teach me something taught me so much, without using words. It was her heart that spoke to me.

Mrs. Johnson

Directly across Randolph Street to the east was Mrs. Johnson's house. She was a widow with ten children. Ruthie, who was the youngest, and Katherine, a few years older than Ruthie, were our trusted baby-sitters. I couldn't pronounce their names properly. I called them "Oochie" and "Khaki." Ruth remembers that when she and Katherine stayed with Elaine and me, we were content if they told us that Mama went to a tea party!

We always addressed Mrs. Johnson just like that, "Mrs. Johnson." I didn't even recall her first name until recently when Auntie Blanche helped me with some details. Her full name was Letha Maude Johnson. She helped Mama with various tasks around the house, and Daddy watched out for her, especially during the war years when her four sons were in the Navy. Everyone on Randolph Street looked out for each other. That wasn't unusual for our small community when I was a kid.

Katherine, Carolyn, age 2, and Ruth

Ruth remembers that Mom made the skirts that Katherine and she are wearing in the above photo, from the fabric of Dad's old suits. Mom was a creative seamstress. Their sweaters were ordered from a catalogue.

Ruth recently shared with me that it was amazing how her mother kept all of her children together after Mr. Johnson passed away in 1931. Ruth was only four years old. Her older sisters, Martha, Zora, and Margaret, were all married by that time. The four sons, Lester, Sam, Burt and Delmar were next in birth order. All four sons joined the Navy during World War II. The three youngest children were Leona, Katherine, and Ruth.

Mrs. Johnson lived in a house that had no indoor plumbing nor running water, just like Derrecky's house. I loved to visit her when she was sitting outside on her front porch. I'd perch myself up on the porch ledge and feel important. She was a good listener.

Katherine played a character role in a play at the high school. Mom and Dad thought I was old enough to go and watch my baby sitter's performance. The name of the play escapes me, but Katherine played a tough, hillbilly female who sat in her chair with her feet up on an open oven door, spitting and smoking a corncob pipe that she held between her teeth.

Katherine, baby John, and Mrs. Johnson

I summed up Khaki's performance in my own words with, "She poked her pipe, and pit." There were a few S sounds missing from the front of my words.

Ruth remembers summer days sitting on a blanket in our back yard helping Mom break green beans. Ruth and Katherine took care of Elaine and me while Mom tended to the many loads of laundry on "warsh day." She remembers lots of little girls' ruffled clothes and Daddy's white shirts hanging on the clothesline, all needing to be carefully ironed the next day.

It has been a treat to reconnect with my baby sitter and former neighbor after all these years and listen to Ruth share stories of her warm memories of growing up on Randolph Street. Ruth now lives in Council Bluffs, Iowa.

There were several mulberry trees on Randolph Street. Elaine and I ate as many berries as we picked, as the photo will confirm. We are in Mrs. Johnson's yard when the above photo was taken. I'm guessing it was Mom who found us like this and bolted for her trusty Kodak camera, her way of saving and sharing memories.

Eating mulberries

In the background is a weeping willow tree. Behind the tree is a small building. The next story happened in that building.

One warm summer day, I decided it was time to take my little sister across the street and show her Mrs. Johnson's outhouse. Elaine was still in a diaper; perhaps she was not yet two years old. It must have been an unusually hot day because a diaper was the only thing that Elaine was wearing. Typical summer attire for wee ones.

I don't remember what actually transpired inside Mrs. Johnson's outhouse, but Elaine still remembers how frightened she was sitting on the edge of the big hole. I can't imagine how I lifted Elaine up onto the seat. It's a miracle that she didn't fall in. God was watching out for us that day. Pinning the diaper back onto my little sister proved to be an impossible task for me. So I gave up and led Elaine out of the outhouse in her birthday suit.

At that moment, Mom realized we had disappeared from our yard, and she began looking for us. In a scene she described often, there we were, heading back home across the street hand in hand. I had Elaine's diaper thrown over one of my arms, and with the other I was leading a completely naked little sister.

I'm grateful that Mom did not let us forget this story, and I'm grateful to Mrs. Johnson for happy memories and for sharing the outhouse with her neighbors.

Grandma's Gifts

Hidden behind the grape arbor,
a row of hollyhocks,
and the clothesline,
was Grandma's garden.

The coolness of the early morning
was the perfect time to be in one
of her favorite places.
I'd watch her rearrange
her oversized, white sunbonnet
with one hand,
while steadying herself
on the hoe handle with the other.

Grandma sometimes talked quietly
to her rows of beans, cabbages,
and Swiss chard,
as she worked the fertile,
black, Iowa soil.

Stiff, aging joints never kept
Grandma from the place
where she connected
with a new day,
her roots and memories,
and her God.

When I tend my flower garden
early "of a morning"
I'm reminded of her
favorite hymn,
"In the Garden."

Escaping the afternoon heat,
Grandma moved her work

to another favorite spot
on the shaded front porch.
It was my favorite place
to be with Grandma.

We'd sit for hours
in the porch swing,
talking,
breaking a *mess* of green beans,
shelling peas, or
sorting gooseberries for a
homemade pie,
Grandma's favorite.
I'd never go home
empty-handed.

These rewards of the land
provided Grandma with
loving opportunities
to give to her family.

My rewards are
these lasting memories.

CHAPTER THREE

The Buildings at 608 Randolph Street

The Shed

The old shed had other names. Sometimes we called it the coal house; sometimes we called it the smoke house. It sat about forty steps outside the back door of the house at *608 Randolph Street.*

After World War II ended, our neighbor, Lester Johnson, came home from his service in the Navy. He approached Daddy and asked to be put to work. Daddy told him that we needed a shed.

The little shed was always painted white. For a time, the shed was used to store the coal that was the fuel used in the old black kitchen cook stove. How relieved Mom was to see that monstrosity leave her kitchen!

Garden tools stood in one corner. There was the manual garden plow that dug one row at a time as Daddy helped Mom get her garden ready for planting. Then Mom followed the hoe, one row at a time and one seed at a time. The assortment of garden tools included various shovels, rakes, and hoes, which Daddy carefully cleaned and oiled to prevent rust.

Old, worn-out furniture and ailing appliances were kept because Daddy always said, "That might be just what we need sometime," or, "You never know when that might come in handy." Mom's old kitchen cabinet with a flour bin, a pull-out work surface, and upper cupboards, no longer looked white and useful, but it had sentimental value, and it lived out its remaining years in the shed. Off-season window screens or storm windows took up space at one end. Many things that couldn't be thrown out, but probably should have, ended up in the shed.

For many years the shed served as a dog house for our terrier, Tippy. His food and water dishes and his bed sat near the door. He would go inside when it got dark, and we would lock the door from the outside, as we told him good night.

The little old shed still stands today.

The Chicken House

West of our home stood a little wooden house with two windows and a door. It was the home of Mom's many chickens. A white picket fence separated our back yard from the chicken yard.

When Mom and Dad were first married, Mom had her own chicken business. She supplied one of the grocery stores in Bedford with freshly cleaned, dressed, cut-up fryers.

It was exciting to go with Mom every spring to the Bedford Hatchery, owned and operated by Bill Hensch and his father-in-law, E.I. Wilson. We'd come home with two or more huge flat boxes of fluffy, yellow, chirping baby chicks. They thrived in the brooder house under the warmth of an electric light bulb. We liked to watch them eat their dry food and drink their water. It wasn't as much fun changing the newspapers beneath the chicks, but it had to be done.

How disappointing it was to see them grow from tiny yellow balls of downy softness into scrawny half-grown chickens with scarcely enough white feathers to cover their bodies.

When they were ready for market, Mom was a whiz at catching and killing the chickens. She used the crowbar method for quick decapitation. Several headless birds would flop around in our back yard at one time. I helped Mom with this assembly line process and can remember disliking it intensely. The scalding process loosened the feathers. This was done by holding the two feet of the headless chicken in one hand while dipping it into a bucket of scalding hot water. This made it easier to remove all of the feathers. After the feathers were all plucked off the bird, the singeing process assured us that no feathers remained. The odor of singed chicken feathers defies description. The chickens were washed thoroughly and placed in a clean metal dishpan, where they awaited their turn to be *dressed*. I wondered why Mom called this whole process one of dressing chickens since it looked pretty obvious to me that they were more undressed than dressed. Mom could dress two dozen chickens in one afternoon, and fry one for dinner that evening. And eat it! All in the same day!

Mom gathered eggs from the nests in the chicken house and traded them at Harbour's Produce downtown.

As Ma and Pa grocery stores dwindled away to make room for the larger chains, Mom discontinued her chicken and egg business.

The little old chicken house was cleaned out. It no longer smelled of chicken feed. Elaine and I decided to turn it into a playhouse. Several coats of bright red, blue, and yellow paint drastically changed the appearance inside the little house. We placed some of our small furniture in the house. A doll bed, miniature sink, stove, table, rocking chair, and a doll buggy took up residence there. When we finally convinced Daddy to let us have a puppy, the little house became the first home for our new terrier, Tippy. He was a lucky little pup. Elaine and I played there a lot, pretending that both Jimmie, age three, and Tippy were our babies. Elaine and I made several attempts to sleep all night in the playhouse, but we never mustered up enough bravery to stay the entire night.

Later, when the playhouse days were over, the little house was moved closer to the barn and became the home of two orphaned lambs named Bounce and Lucy.

Eventually the little chicken house was taken down. The white picket fence was taken away. Grass was planted, and the former chicken yard became merely an extension of the west edge of the back yard, where four walnut trees grow today.

The One Car Garage

Sometime in the 50s we had a one car garage built. It stood at the west end of the driveway. It was an unpretentious little building, with its gray siding, two windows and a normal sized garage door. It was just the right size for our games of Andy Andy Over. During long summer evenings when it stayed light until 9 P.M., a group of friends would toss the ball back and forth over the building until darkness set in.

The garage had lots of storage space above the rafters where Mom and Dad kept things that should have been taken to the dump. For a few years we kept our rabbit cage in the garage. The cage was the home of Magic, a large copper-colored pet rabbit. Magic was given to me at a Magician show that was held in the high school auditorium. Harold Wilson, a classmate in my fifth grade class, and I were called up to the stage. We participated in an act of magical wonder, and I still wonder what happened. Harold and I were suddenly changed from one costume into another. The back-stage helper probably had something to do with the magic! For our help in the act, the magician presented each of us with a live rabbit.

The green 1949 Ford was kept in the garage longer than any other car. In another chapter I have related the unfortunate event that changed the appearance of both the Ford and the garage.

The little gray garage was taken down after serving us well for nearly half of a century, and today the sidewalk that used to connect the garage with the house leads to nowhere.

The Old Red Barn

A typical day in 1945

The old red barn sits on the quiet acreage behind the big house at *608 Randolph Street*. The barn roof is sagging a bit in the center. The rough wood reveals the age of the building. The fresh coat of red paint shows it off proudly, even though it leans slightly to the south. The path from the barnyard gate to the barn door is worn and sunken into the rich black soil. Surrounding the barn is the barnyard where several friendly animals graze.

"Watch your step, Girls," Daddy warns us as Elaine and I follow closely behind him to the barn door. He places the old metal milk bucket inside the barn. He lifts the one-legged milk stool off the hook where cobwebs have multiplied for years. We know the routine. Daddy looks down the lane to the west and calls for the Jersey milk cows.

"Here Boss. Here Babe."

Elaine and I try to mimic Daddy's cattle call. We laugh at our attempts to sound grown up. Within a short time, the Jersey cows amble slowly up the lane toward the old red barn.

The setting sun warms the already hot, humid, summer day. The steamy stillness in the air is accompanied by the sounds of crickets in the tall grass, the rustling noises of hens in the nearby hen house, and the soft cooing of mourning doves finding comfort in the tall shade trees. An Iowa summer can be unmercifully long and hot, yet there's something magical about it. The daylight lingers until 9 P.M. and the lightning bugs dance around the yard waiting for children to catch them.

As the cows obediently walk single file through the barn door, Elaine and I are amazed to see each one go to the same stall day after day.

"Daddy, how can you sit on the one legged milking stool and not fall off?" we want to know. Daddy patiently explains that with practice it becomes easy.

"Can we look in the saddle room? Can we go up to the hay mow, Daddy?"

We love the rich aroma of the leather saddles and bridles, but our favorite spot is the haymow. Two little girls scampering up the crude ladder resemble monkeys climbing in jungle trees.

The earthy smells of a haymow cannot be found anywhere else on earth. We love to climb up onto the stacked bales of hay looking down from the top with a sense of great accomplishment. Some of the bales have been broken, ready to be sent below to the food bin. Elaine and I love to roll in it, pile it high, jump into it again and again, laughing and giggling all the while. The hay covers our clothes and sticks to our skin and hair. Finding a piece of rope, we delight in throwing it high over a rafter and tying it into a Tarzan and Jane swing. We take turns flying through the huge expanse of the barn's dusty space and jumping into the hay below.

As we rearrange the hay, we find an unexpected surprise, a litter of baby kittens not more than three weeks old. Their eyes are barely open. They tumble over each other hoping to find their mother. Their tiny voices cry out in unison.

"Wonder which barn cat they belong to?" I ask. We are anxious to share our discovery with Daddy, but he does not seem very surprised.

Elaine and I know that if we handle them, the mother cat will surely move her little family. But how can we not touch those tiny, soft bodies lying in the stiff straw. If the mother cat allows it, we will have her kittens tamed in no time.

Daddy calls up to us, reminding us to stop jumping around. We are right above the milking room, and hay is falling through the cracks of the old floorboards into the bucket of fresh milk. The cows are swatting at the falling debris with their tails.

Several barn cats and even the tame cats sit around the milking room waiting for Daddy to squirt a stream of milk in their direction. They jump around erratically, catching the milk in their mouths in mid-air, like feline jumping beans.

"Daddy, can we ride Smokey, please, just for a little while?" we ask.

"Only until suppertime" is his answer, as he saddles and bridles the small horse and helps us up into the saddle. We ride to the far end of the pasture and let Smokey gallop back to the barn. Truth be known, we probably couldn't have changed Smokey's mind or direction, even if we wanted to. Suppertime is 6P.M. sharp, every evening, like most of the people in town.

With our horse ride completed, Elaine and I run along beside Daddy as he carries the aluminum bucket of milk to the back porch. Welcoming aromas are emanating from the kitchen and we realize that Mom is frying bacon, probably for BLTs, a favorite supper. Our family eats every meal together, every day.

We watch Daddy pour the milk into the big round container at the top of the separating machine on the back porch. We know the whole milk will exit through the big faucet and the rich cream will come from the little one. We wait for our taste of warm milk with as much anticipation as did the cats in the barn. Elaine and I giggle about the thick, warm, milk mustaches on our upper lips as we anxiously wait for Mama to announce, "Supper's ready!"

Watercolor painting by Carolyn

The House

The photograph of the old Scherich house appeared in *Centennial History, Bedford, Iowa, 1953* and was shown as one of the early houses built in Bedford.

The original floor plan of the house at 608 Randolph Street resembled a cross like the Red Cross symbol, but it doesn't resemble that anymore. Rooms were added. Windows were changed into doors, and doors into windows. The chimneys are gone, and the vines and ivy no longer trail up the sides of the house. The inside and outside have been drastically changed.

A wrap-around front porch was part of the earlier house. White columns with gingerbread trim gave the porch a welcoming façade, typical of an earlier time. The balcony above the porch provided a great view of the town as well as relief from the heat on a hot summer night. In dire need of much repair, the porch was taken off in the summer of 1954. Stripped of the porch, the front never again had the stately appeal that defined old houses built during that era.

The few original physical features that still remain are the tall narrow windows, etched glass in the outer doors, arched ceilings in the second story, hardwood floors, a limestone foundation that will probably last another one hundred years, a few light switches and old fixtures, and the rather steep gables.

With the additions, the house became a ten room house with seven closets.

As a little kid on a tricycle, I could ride from room to room in a complete circle. Before a furnace was installed in the basement, we closed off a couple of rooms in the wintertime, and my circular tricycle path was interrupted until the return of warmer weather.

My favorite room was the kitchen where Mama's big, black coal stove filled up a corner, heated the room, and cooked our food. The large, black stovepipe trailed upward before bending into the corner and out of the house. This was replaced by a modern electric range at the end of World War II. It didn't matter what Mama used for cooking; the tempting aromas from her red and white kitchen made it a welcome place for a kid to play. In the hot summer months, Mama cooked on a propane gas range that sat on the adjoining back porch. The refrigerator was also on the back porch until the coal stove was removed from the kitchen. After that, a small Crosley-Shelvador refrigerator took its place on the west wall of the kitchen. Mom's kitchen was highly inefficient but fairly common in the 1930s and 40s.

During the summer months the kitchen was filled with a variety of aromas as Mama canned hundreds of jars of garden vegetables and fruit. Several large crocks sat near the back door for weeks while Mom made her wonderful dill pickles, bread and butter pickles, green tomato relish, and cabbage-stuffed green bell peppers. Those aromas lingered for days after the canning process was finished, and the filled Mason jars were neatly arranged on shelves in the basement.

Next to the kitchen is the dining room. Mom and Daddy started housekeeping with their large scale Jacobean style table, chairs, and buffet. This room was the scene of thousands of family dinners, served family style. Daddy always sat at the south end of the long table and solemnly said the table grace before the meals. Mom sat at the opposite end of the table near the kitchen door. Sunday dinner was a special time with several regular guests who became part of the family.

Elaine and I played under the large wooden dining room table when we were small. The supports from each table leg met in the center where a rectangular space was just large enough for two little girls to play make believe. Sometimes the space was a car, sometimes a boat, sometimes a house.

During school years, we pulled out the extension leaves at each end of the table to create separate desks. Hundreds of reports and pages of homework and letters were written at these spots. Most days one of Daddy's typewriters could be seen on the table. He typed his sermons, funeral and wedding messages, and various reports for several organizations in town.

The bathroom next to the kitchen had a large deep bathtub with a wide rounded rim. It did not have claw-feet like Grandma's tub, but it stood tall in the room. During our long baths, Elaine and I soaped the top rim of our bathtub to make it slippery. We'd sit on the edge and propel ourselves around the tub. More soap meant we could go faster. We didn't have a staircase or banister to slide down, so we created our own fun by sliding around on the rim of the bathtub. On Saturday nights we could hear the kitchen radio playing the music from *The Saturday Night Barn Dance Frolic*.

Our bedrooms were upstairs. Elaine and I shared the south bedroom for many years. Eventually we got twin beds. When I was thirteen years old, I decided to move to the north bedroom. During our high school years, Elaine and I had our own bedrooms. When baby Jimmie came along, he had a room at the top of the stairs. A green Hopalong Cassidy chenille bedspread covered his youth bed. After Elaine left home, Jim moved into the south bedroom. During all of the shifting around, Mom and Daddy kept the east bedroom upstairs for over sixty years. From their east window they had a clear view of the court house clock and the rolling hills of southern Iowa.

The walls were always wallpapered. There were many, many layers of wallpaper. The woodwork was always painted white.

Later, new ceiling tiles replaced the wallpapered ceilings. The hardwood floors were eventually covered with carpeting sometime in the 1950s.

Other changes were made. The back porch and kitchen walls were paneled. An upstairs bathroom was added. The downstairs bathroom was remodeled. Central air-conditioning and heating were added. Black shutters were added to the exterior windows. Numerous minor improvements were made. The original house has been drastically changed.

When my brother, sister and I sorted through our parents' accumulation of things, Dad's favorite manual typewriter was declared a keeper. Jim has given it a place of honor in his home. It sits on a typewriter table, complete with the first letter that Dad typed on it. The letter was written to Mom, thanking her for the typewriter. Written in January 1934, six months before they married, Daddy remained true to his conservative display of affection with this closing: *Sincerely, Carl.*

On the day of the final household sale, the furniture was carried out to the lawn. Elaine told me that the hardest thing to see was the dining room table, the chairs, and the buffet leaving their home of sixty-nine years. We have hundreds of photographs of family and friends around that table.

A year or so before Daddy passed away, we were talking about the old house, its history and its possible future. His words were, "The old house won't bring very much money, but it's tight, and it will make a comfortable home for someone, someday."

Well, Daddy, it is making a comfortable home for Jeff and Tara and your namesake, Tristen Carl Cummings. Life goes on.

Another generation is calling it home.

The Music of the Sunset

The large back yard of
my childhood home
dips to the west,
where the horizon
meets the evening sky.

From there, high on the hill
a front row seat welcomes
the viewer to see and hear
the sights and sounds of
the music of the sunset.

The gentle highs and lows
of the fertile hills to the west
weave a pattern
of rhythmic design
beneath the fading sunlight.

Rows of trees and fence posts
dance along from left to right
across rolling pastures
like running notes on a score of music
up and down and up again.

After the sun has made its slow descent
behind the landscape
the light prevails for a time,
and in this latent afterglow
the still countryside
sings Nature's sweetest lullaby.

Serene and quiescent
the fading light composes
a shadowy background
for the fireflies and crickets to add
their final notes to the day.

Twilight melts into darkness
As another day sings
the final notes
in the hushed finale
of the music of the sunset.

*Photographs taken by Carolyn from the back yard
at 608 Randolph Street*

CHAPTER FOUR

Family History

The Courtship of Carl and Helen

Mama lived in the country. Daddy lived in town. They were destined to meet while playing their clarinets in the Bedford City Band. Mama was twenty-one years old; Daddy was twenty. They had their first date in November of 1927. The movie that they saw on that first date was *My Best Pal*. It was playing at the Bedford Rialto Theater down on Main Street.

It was quite a distance for Daddy to drive to pick up Mama. She lived ten miles west of Bedford on the O'Dell family farm. He would drive either the family Overland Touring car or his own 1923 Model T Ford. Mud or gravel roads made driving a real challenge. That year, Mama was the teacher at the Timberlake School near her family's farm.

Mama's younger brother, Herman, became fast friends with Daddy. Grandpa Lester O'Dell said, "Carl wooed Herman and married Helen." Uncle Herman and Daddy were close friends, even before they became brothers-in-law.

Mama just happened to meet Doris Lucas at Bedford High School in 1922. Doris and Helen were the smallest girls in their class. They were both taking Normal Training classes, hoping to become future teachers. Their friendship developed and it was just a matter of time before Doris met Helen's brother, Herman.

The courtship of Carl and Helen cannot be told without giving equal time to the developing friendship of

Herman and Doris. Now there was a foursome! They laughed together on picnics, at the Chautauqua shows and at the movies. They went on trips together, usually taking two cars. They improved the clarinet and saxophone section in the Bedford City Band when Saturday night concerts were given in the band-stand in the court yard and in the high school auditorium.

Mama and Doris went to college in Cedar Falls, Iowa, in September of 1928. After graduation, they went wherever they could find a teaching position, which in those years were precious few. The friendship between Mom and Daddy, as well as Doris and Herman, became a long distant one for a few years.

After several years of teaching, Mom wanted to hear wedding bells instead of school bells. Daddy, in his conservative wisdom, calculated the high cost of marriage during and after the depression. He was established as a cashier at the Bedford National Bank. But Mom was ready to exchange her teaching attire for a housedress, the uniform of married women in the 1930s and 40s.

When Daddy finally asked Mama to marry him, she was ready. They had dated almost seven years.

Mama resigned her teaching position in Villisca, Iowa, in the spring of 1934. They were married at the Methodist Parsonage in Bedford on July 8th. Naturally, the couple who witnessed their wedding was Herman and Doris, whose own wedding would take place eleven months later.

Mom and Daddy went to Lake Okoboji, Iowa's popular lake resort, for their honeymoon.

Wedding picture of Carl and Helen
From left: Herman O'Dell, Carl, Helen, Doris Lucas

Back home in Bedford, they lived in a little house on Court Street for a couple of months before moving to the acreage on Randolph Street. For the next sixty-five years they experienced all the highs and lows, joy and pain, of long lives cemented together with *lots of love*.

The photograph of the Bedford City Band, on the next page, was among the treasures that we found in the house. As always, Daddy had documented it well, including the names of each band member on the back of the photograph.

The Bedford City Band *(1927) after a band concert in the Bedford High School Auditorium.*

Seated from left to right: Herman O'Dell, Mrs. Walden Weaver, Carl Cummings, Billy Richardson, John Harold Meikle, Helen O'Dell, Gayle Howe, Warren Mitchell (director), Eula Jefferies, Ed Scott, Clella Mitchell, Jack Thompson, Clyde Perkins, Beryle Rhoads, Verla Streebin, Roy W. McLain, Maxine Kopp, Esther Hollaway Dinges.

Standing from left to right: Ralph W. Thompson, John Swap, A. J. Bridges, Tommy McLaury, L.C. Sid Morris, Frederick Weiser, Waldon Weaver, Harley E. Nelson, J. Frank Thummel.

Daddy's Parents

Not too many kids today have the privilege of growing up next door to their grandparents. Grandma Florence and Grandpa Clyde's yard was next to ours, with no fence or divider to separate us. At almost any time, day or night, Grandma was home. I visited her often.

Grandma Florence's words come back to me again and again. I know they are hers. No one else said them, and I don't know where Grandma found them.

Grandma often said that she had an "i dee," (accent the I) or idea. "I have an idee. We'll go dreckly to the kitchen and get you a sugar cookie," she'd say. *Dreckly* was another favorite word of Grandma's.

The word "allowed" was shortened and grandma-ized to "lowd." She might say something like, "I lowd as if I'd take an apple pie to the church." Her word for a chicken or turkey wishbone was "pulley bone."

Grandma made the thickest sugar cookies I have ever seen. She'd let me dip flour from the flour bin of her kitchen cabinet. Then we'd add the sugar and other ingredients. Before baking these thick round circles of dough, Grandma piled lots of granulated sugar on top of each one. For many years she had a black coal stove in her kitchen. The black stovepipe stretched overhead from the east wall to the west and out the chimney hole in the ceiling. It gave heat to the kitchen in summer as well as winter. When we finished our baking, I'd help her "warsh and rench" the dishes.

I spent a lot of time with my grandparents when I was three and four, old enough to go next door alone, and before Elaine became my little shadow. It seemed like my second home.

As a child, I didn't think about Grandma's homespun vernacular as anything unusual, in fact, I didn't think about it at all! She was my Grandma and I loved her and knew that she loved her family very much. As I get older, I cherish the times we had together and the vocabulary that she left us.

She was the main babysitter for Elaine and Jimmie and me. We knew that there were just certain routines that happened only at Grandma and Grandpa's house. One was the "scrappeed" apple treat. After cutting an apple in half, Grandma fed us as though we were little birds with no teeth. She would slide the tip of a blade of a table knife across the cut fruit collecting a tiny amount of apple, then she'd place it in our mouths. We'd close our lips over the knife as Grandma slid it out. The apple took on a definite metallic taste, but we would never tell Grandma. This was a favorite way to eat apples, only at Grandma's house, and long after we had teeth. Sometimes Grandma gave us her bread treats. One was a slice of bread in a bowl with milk poured over it. Another one was a generous supply of granulated sugar sprinkled over a slice of fresh buttered bread. These treats were reserved for Grandma's house only.

Grandma was always complimentary of Mom's cooking. She appreciated an invitation to "come cross the yard" to 608 for a meal, especially after Grandpa died.

"My! Helen, I believe this is the best apple pie you've ever made. It's extree good," she'd say.

We knew Grandma loved homemade ice cream and would give her a generous helping before asking if she could use another scoop. She'd always say, "Yes, I believe I can get it down." And could she ever!

With her large picnic basket on her arm, she'd leave the house for the afternoon. Grandpa would drive her to her destination, which was the Baptist Church down on Main Street. That's the only place that grandmas could go alone. There she'd keep the conversation alive as she quilted with her Ladies Aide Society. They worshiped together upstairs, they shared their food in the downstairs parlor and kitchen, and they quilted in the tiny room at the bottom of the stairs in the church basement.

Anchored to the quilting stretchers would be a quilt in progress. Its pieces had been lovingly hand-stitched together to complete the top of the quilt. Between the top and the lining was a layer of batting. Sometimes Grandma carded her own wool, which became the batting or stuffing for a cozy winter quilt or a tied comforter. Several Grandma-type ladies sat around the quilt frame stitching designs upon the handmade work of art. One hand directed the needle over the top, and the other beneath the quilt, caught each series of tiny stitches and directed the needle above for the next ones. I learned that a good quilter tries to get seven minute stitches on the needle. Their needles, called *betweens* were extremely small with a tiny round eye which held the thread. While they worked, their conversation never lagged. I could tell they cared about each other. They helped hand-quilt a quilt for anyone who had a new top ready to be finished. This kept their hands busy as they talked. I think this was their therapy as they listened to one another and shared the events of their lives and families. These were women who had known each other all of their lives. They worked things out with her group of ladies at the quilting bee. I'm pretty sure that they threw a little gossip into their day, too, but you didn't hear it from me!

Sometimes Elaine and I would go there after school if Mom wasn't home. There we would crawl around on the floor beneath the big quilt frame. Fascinated with the several pairs of busy hands, we would listen to the ladies as they shared their words of wisdom. We understood that this beautiful craft was much more than pieces of cloth and stitches; it embraced the many lives that were pieced together with needle and thread.

All Grandmas wore the same kind of sturdy, laced-up oxford shoes. Their baggy nylons looked uncomfortable and hot in the summer. A cotton print ankle-length housedress was the usual attire.

When it was time to end the quilting project for the day, the ladies opened their picnic baskets, bringing out beautiful homemade pies and cookies. The aroma of freshly brewed coffee filled the kitchen along with their compliments to each other. Elaine and I never missed an invitation to enjoy refreshments served at the end of the quilting bee. Where else could a kid get so much attention along with an after-school snack? And Grandma had a chance to show off her granddaughters before Mom's taxi service arrived to take us home.

Grandma's popcorn popper was a forerunner of the hot-air corn popper. A long-handled wire basket with a slide-back lid held the kernels of corn. The source of heat came from her black coal stove, and later, from her modern electric range. We'd turn the burner to the hottest temperature and shake the wire basket over the heat. Fantastic popcorn! Then a hot stream of melted butter was poured over the bowl of corn, followed by just the right amount of salt. We never made it any other way at Grandma's house.

Today, Jim proudly displays Grandma's wire basket corn popper beside the fireplace in his newly remodeled basement family room. It looks perfectly at home there. It belongs in that house and in that spot.

In one of the upstairs bedrooms of Grandma and Grandpa's house was a featherbed mattress made by Grandma. It was in the east bedroom, the one that had been Daddy's room when he still lived with his parents. The brown metal bed presented a stark contrast to the softness of the deep loft of the featherbed mattress. Elaine and I weren't the only kids that loved to jump on that bed. We invited our friends, neighbors, and cousins to join us. And, the best part was, Grandma never scolded us when we left the bed in disarray.

A large weeping willow tree stood outside their back porch door. Grandpa used the branches to make whistles. He'd sit on the front porch and quietly whittle them out with his pocketknife, and then take pleasure in watching Elaine and me blow reedy sounds from them. Grandma always threatened us in her playful way by saying, "I'll make a willow switch and swat 'ya on the behind, you little splinter." She never did, of course. Only rarely would Grandma reprimand us with her soft words of admonishment such as, "There was no call to do that now, Honey," or, "You didn't go to do that on purpose, did you."

When a breeze touched the willow tree, it moved like it was dancing, swaying back and forth, the leaves touching each other with soothing sounds, as the long, lazy branches bowed to the ground.

Behind Grandma's wire clotheslines stood a handsome row of hollyhocks. My friends and I liked to make dancing dolls from the flowers. We would stack several different colored blossoms on a toothpick and twirl them about, imitating the colorful skirt of a Flamingo dancer. An unopened bud perched on the top end of the toothpick became the head of the doll. When I see hollyhocks, I'm reminded of those treasured innocent days in my Grandma's flower garden.

Grandma loved working in her vegetable garden "of a morning" when it was cool. Her huge white sunbonnet protected her fair skin from the sun. As she bent over her garden hoe, she quietly hummed and sang her favorite hymns, as though she was encouraging her plants to grow. Her favorite hymn was "In the Garden." The words of that timeless hymn, sung at her funeral, gave comfort to our family.

"And He walks with me,
and He talks with me,
and he tells me I am His own.
And the joy we share as we tarry there,
none other has ever known."

I love that old hymn and always think of Grandma when I hear it.

In the summer time, Grandma and Grandpa sat outside on their front porch until dark. It was always a place we could go for unconditional love.

Sometimes Elaine and I would sing a duet or *speak a piece* of poetry for Grandma and Grandpa. They were always an encouraging audience. Otherwise, Grandma usually kept the conversation moving as she covered dozens of topics of conversations. Grandpa and Elaine and I mostly listened. Grandma's laugh was no more than a titter but sometimes her sense of humor would show through when she'd start a story with "I have to tell you a joke on Grandma."

Grandpa chewed tobacco and would occasionally get up from his chair, go to the edge of the porch, and spit. We were used to this. Just a fact of life. The other fact about Grandpa was that he always listened to the market reports on the radio at noon; they were especially important before a sale of livestock and hogs at the sale barn down on Main Street. There was a sale there every Saturday, where my Grandpa Clyde and our Randolph Street neighbor, Ivan Wells, shouted out the auctioneer's cry.

Grandpa had a few milk cows, and sometimes he raised pigs. We'd see him walk from the back porch in route to his red barn with an empty metal milk bucket. When he finished milking the cows, he carried the full bucket to the back porch and poured the milk into the top of a large metal separator. Elaine and I would sit beside Grandpa and wait for the first warm milk to stream from the spout into the containers. Grandma brought small drinking glasses to the porch for us, since she always "lowd" as if we'd like to sample the warm milk.

"If 'a body' just took the time to sort these old pictures, you wouldn't have so much stuff to go through someday, Carl," Grandma said one day. It turned out that Grandma was the "body" that carefully organized and labeled each important family picture for safekeeping. Daddy chuckled as he looked through the box of old photos, long after Grandma went to meet her Maker. On the back of one picture Grandma had written this: "Carl, I don't have any idea who these people are. You can toss this one." Could it be that she had some of those saver and keeper genes too?

The last car that Grandpa owned was a black 1940 Ford. He drove it to sales around the county and to the sale barn at the east end of Main Street every Saturday, and, of course, to the Baptist Church every Sunday. That's why it had unbelievably low mileage on it when Daddy inherited it in 1960. Daddy cleaned it, shined it, decorated it, and drove it in several parades on the 4th of July. Aunt Blanche drove it in one of Bedford's parades; said she'd never drive that car again. Dad kept the old Ford registered and insured. When Daddy could no longer drive the car, his grandson, Jeff, drove it in the parade. It just keeps going from one generation to the next, as long as it has a supply of gasoline.

The old car has a new purpose now. It carried passengers to the new pond in the west pasture on Sunday, July 31st, 2005, the day of the Cummings reunion. Either Jim or Jeff acted as chauffeurs and made several runs to the pond with curious family members.

Grandpa Clyde was an auctioneer. I loved to hear his auctioneer cry. He taught my dad the words, perhaps thinking he would follow in his career path. Elaine and Jim and I learned the warm up cry from Daddy.

It goes something like this:

Higgano, Riggano, Hilly Go Landigo

Hickey Kak Kook, Hi Billy Walligo,

Skip to My Loo.

Grandpa was, otherwise, a quiet man. At home, I guess he had to be. I always "lowd" as if my Grandma could carry her end of a conversation a long, long ways and back again!

Grandpa passed away at home in June of 1960. We were all near his bed when he died. My Dad did something that I'll never forget. He sat down on the side of Grandpa's bed, reached over to Grandpa's hand, took his pulse, then as though he was giving a eulogy, he said, "He taught me how to live and he showed me how to die."

Then, as always, Grandma found comfort in the scriptures. Many times she would repeat favorite Psalms aloud, showing us that her strength came from the Lord. Her Bible was often found beside her chair with her reading glasses lying across the open pages.

Elaine and I took turns staying at night with Grandma for several weeks after Grandpa's death. Since we had college classes in Maryville, Missouri, the next morning, we had to get up early. Grandma always got up earlier. She would go to the kitchen and boil up some of her strong coffee. The coffee grounds and cold water were measured into her aluminum coffee pot and placed on her electric range to boil. During the boiling process the smell of strong coffee could wake up the entire west end of town. Just before serving it, Grandma added a cup or two of cold water. The grounds settled to the bottom and the coffee tasted just right. The early morning wake-up calls and Grandma's strong coffee are difficult to forget.

Grandma stayed in her home, the house at 704 Randolph Street, for the next ten years. She was able to *keep house* and *do for herself* as she would say. In spite of some physical limitations, she loved being in her home. Daddy and Mom were her main caregivers for those years. Aunt Blanche came frequently to visit and help.

Only three months after Grandpa's death, I graduated from college and secured my first teaching position in Denver, Colorado. The morning that I left 608 Randolph Street, we were loading my belongings into Daddy's car with the overflow filling Uncle Wilbur and Aunt Neva's camper. Grandma walked across the yard through the dewy grass to see us off. Her parting words of wisdom have encouraged me over and over again. She said, "Honey, all those people in the big city are just friends you haven't met yet."

She knew that my strength, also, came from the Lord. I called on Him often and remembered Grandma's words. They got me through lots of unfamiliar journeys and uncertain times.

Our Song

You are my sunshine, my only sunshine
You make me happy when skies are gray

It was our song.
My Grandpa sang it to me
in his deep bass voice
when I was three.

Sometimes Grandpa would
whistle our song.
He tried to teach me
how to whistle.
I couldn't whistle
when I was three.

You'll never know, dear
how much I love you
Please don't take my sunshine away.

I loved sitting on his lap
feeling his deep voice
vibrate through his chest and
looking in the pockets
of his bib coveralls.

The snaps were a shiny copper color and
each one had a letter engraved on it.
But I couldn't read
when I was three.

When I went to my
grandparents' house
next door
I could usually find Grandpa
in the living room
in his big tan overstuffed chair.
He had kind brown eyes and a bald head.
I'd crawl up into his big lap and feel loved.
He didn't smile often, but he always
smiled at me,
when I was three.

Grandpa's favorite kind of candy
was in the candy dish that sat
on the big lace-covered
dining room table.
Sugar coated orange slices
were a special treat
for me
when I was three.

Sixty years later
I became a grandmother.
I rocked my infant granddaughter
as she cuddled close to me
on my shoulder,
and I sang our song

You are my sunshine
My only sunshine

And remembered a time
not so long ago
when my Grandpa sang to me
when I was three.

Mama's Parents

Mama called her parents Papa and Mama. They lived on the O'Dell farm ten miles west of Bedford on Iowa Highway 2. When Mama would say to Daddy, "I'd like to drive out to the farm tonight and see Mama and Papa," he'd never turn down her request. This made me happy since a visit to the farm meant time to play with cousins Cheryl and Keith, who lived in the newer farmhouse next door.

Grandpa, Lester Loren O'Dell, married Grandma, Emma May Fitch, on March 5, 1890, and they established the family farm west of Bedford. There, they raised their four children, two sons and two daughters. Uncle Bruce and Aunt Neva were a year apart in age, born in 1899 and 1900. My mother was born in 1906. The youngest child was Herman, who came along two years later. Mama idolized her older sister, Neva, and played with her younger brother, Herman.

Bruce, Herman, Helen, Neva

Circa 1909

Grandma O'Dell's tiny kitchen was sparsely equipped with a work table, a cabinet or cupboard, and a cook stove. An icebox sat in the corner of the dark room. The family always ate meals at the round oak table in the adjoining dining room, the coziest room in the house. A stove, which stood along the north wall, heated the room in the winter. Grandpa's big wooden rocking chair sat in the northeast corner, not far from the stove. An oak telephone hung on the wall above his chair. Grandma sat in a smaller rocking chair on the other side of the stove. She wasn't quite five feet tall and was thick around the middle. Her long white hair was twisted into a bun on top of her head. I don't remember seeing Grandma wear anything other than her ankle length, loose fitting dresses.

The loud ticking of the mantel clock is a sound etched in my memory. It sat up on a shelf on the west wall of the dining room, and its mellow chime reminded us of the hour. I liked to watch Grandma wind the clock with that special key, making sure the pendulum could swing freely. The rhythms of the creaking old rockers played in sync with the ticking of the clock. They created a relaxing reverie of sounds, which was an important part of the whole experience of being in my grandparents' house.

When we drove into the driveway, Grandpa would sometimes meet us at the east door. With both arms open, he'd offer giant hugs for Elaine and me. Then we'd sit on his lap and play with the pockets and snaps on his bib coveralls. With each hug, I'd feel a brush of Grandpa's mustache, the first man I knew who had one! Grandpa seemed happy to see us, and we felt loved when we sat on his lap. Grandma was the serious one. She remained distant and austere. I don't remember ever sitting on her lap. She cared for her family in a different way, without an outward display of emotions.

Grandpa stood a foot taller than Grandma. His slender body emphasized his height. Deep set eyes and bushy eyebrows and mustache were the features that I remember. Grandpa eventually became bald on top.

Beneath the white exterior paint on their farmhouse was solid walnut. The lumber came from the timber near by.

Lester and Emma May O'Dell

Mid-1930s

The house had no indoor plumbing nor electricity. It seemed dark even with the kerosene lamp burning on the round, oak table.

Through a doorway from the dining room was a set of steps that made a sudden turn to the right. Bedrooms and a small hallway were on the second floor. A pair of coveralls, the uniform of every farmer, usually hung on a wall hook in one bedroom, long after Grandpa no longer slept upstairs. Each bedroom was furnished with a bed and dresser set constructed of solid walnut, a large trunk, perhaps a rocking chair, and a small night table. Sheer lace panels hung from the windows. The upstairs space was seldom used after all the kids left home.

Next to the cozy dining room downstairs was a larger living room, or a parlor. Not a heated room, it was a favorite sitting room in the summer. On the old roll top desk, we could locate our favorite source of entertainment: the stereoscope. Through the viewer we watched the postcard-sized stereographs come to life in three dimensional clarity.

Adjoining the living room, seeming to be almost an afterthought, was a tiny bedroom. One twin size bed was positioned under the east window. Large dark trunks sat along the dark wallpapered walls.

In his younger years, Uncle Herman did quite a lot of sleep-walking and talking. According to one story that Mama told, Uncle Herman jumped from a second story window in his sleep, and without waking up, he walked upstairs and went back to bed. Uncle Herman was a colorful character!

Back row, Left to right: Lester, Herman, and Bruce
Front row, Left to right: Helen, Neva, and Emma May

A wide, plank walkway stretched the entire length of the house on the north side. Two doorways led to the outside, one from the kitchen and the other from the cozy dining room. A few feet away from the dining room door stood a smoke house, the outhouse, and the milking shed. Behind the shed was the pump over the well, where buckets of water were filled and carried into the house. Just outside the kitchen door was a fruit cellar, that cool, damp, dark place with unfamiliar noises and cobwebs. The best part of visiting the cellar was leaving in a hurry.

Grandpa Lester had his own method of surviving the hot summer evenings. He would lie down on the cool grass in the front yard until his body temperature had cooled down.

Grandpa had three sisters and two brothers. The oldest siblings, Mary, Annazella, and Warren, were born in Ohio and Indiana. Grandpa was the fourth child of Clark O'Dell and Mary Nichols. He was born in Taylor County, Iowa, where he lived all of his life. His younger brother, Leonadus and sister, Alora Ellen were also born in Taylor County, Iowa. Alora died at the age of seven.

The reason that Grandpa O'Dell's fingers on his left hand were shorter than the right hand was the result of a childhood accident. Mama told me about it. When Grandpa was only four years old, he was involved in an incident with an axe. It makes my blood chill to think of that accident. All kinds of emotions arise, from the guilt of the adult who was responsible, to the trauma felt by the child. But when I was a kid, I never gave it much thought. It was just a fact of life that Grandpa O'Dell and my Daddy had matching left hands, both having experienced the accidental loss of part of their fingers on that hand.

My grandma's mother was Sarah Elizabeth Hawley, from Buck Hollow, Vermont. She married Jabez Huntington Fitch in 1857. Jabez came from a family of eight children and they represent the seventh generation of the Fitch family in America. From the records of the *Heralds in London* the genealogy of the Fitch family is quite well documented.

Like all brave pioneers, Sarah Elizabeth and Jabez started westward from Vermont with two young sons, in an oxen-drawn covered wagon. Their oldest son, Lyman Hawley, was born in 1858. The second son, John Ashley, was born in 1863. Most likely, this young couple never expected to see their parents and siblings again. That required courage, faith, and an unending passion for adventure and a better life. They got as far west as Illinois where they stayed for a few years.

Emma May and her sister, Eloise, were born in Belvedere, Illinois. Eloise was born in 1866. Emma May was born on January 25, 1867. Young Eloise died at a young age while the family lived in Illinois, before they moved westward to Taylor County, Iowa.

Left to right: Jabez Fitch with three of his four children: Lyman, Emma May and Arthur. John Ashley was in China.

The youngest child, Arthur May was born in 1875, the only child in that family born in Taylor County.

Grandma, Emma May, was only sixteen years old when her mother died. Sarah Elizabeth died in her forties, leaving a family of four children. The youngest child was only eight years old.

Emma May probably took over many responsibilities after her mother died. When she was 19, her father remarried. Grandma used to tell me that her stepmother often told her that "she didn't eat enough to keep a bird alive." Other than that one line, she never mentioned her stepmother. Emma May's life was a hard life, just as her mother's was. Grandma was skilled in caring for sick neighbors, staying with them for days if conditions warranted. Those brave pioneer men and women experienced hardship and sadness as a part of life. They were risk-takers, and they have my respect and admiration.

Grandma's brother, John Ashley, was a Presbyterian missionary in Chu Fou Shentung, China, for forty years. Only one of their four children, Hugh, survived childhood at the time of China's Boxer Rebellion. Grandma spoke often of this brother, whom she seldom saw. A few fragile letters that she received from him have found a safe place in an antique chest in my home.

As Grandpa Lester's health declined, a double bed was moved into the sitting room downstairs. Grandma slept in her tiny bedroom to be nearby. Grandpa died in his bed on August 5, 1945. His lifetime spanned from the Civil War era to the end of World War II. My aunts and uncles gathered at the farm house on the morning of Grandpa's death, and the only thing that I remember was Grandma's repetitious statement, almost as though she was eulogizing him: "He loved the children so; he loved the children so."

Grandma Emma May O'Dell stayed at her farm home alone in the summer months, but lived with her children during the winters. She broke her hip in a fall, which confined her to a wheelchair for the remainder of her life. She still had her eyesight and ability to crochet and read.

Grandma turned out antimacassars, doilies, and crocheted pillow case edges by the dozens. As long as her children supplied her with crochet thread, she made delicate works of art, much of the time without a pattern.

My cousin, Louise, youngest child of Uncle Wilbur and Aunt Neva, wrote a poem about Grandma's crocheting. With her permission, this is her poem:

Picots and Pineapples

Grandma O'Dell didn't knit, didn't tat,

but crocheted endlessly as she sat.

Picots and pineapples adorned her wares,

doilies, runners, antimacassars for armchairs,

sheets and pillow cases trimmed with her skill,

extra edgings and doilies boxes did fill.

Daddy shook his head and marveled aloud

at her prodigious production, and vowed,

"Just measure it all, and you'll see that I'm right.

She's crocheted enough to fence eighty acres

rabbit-tight!"

By Louise Novinger Merkle

Grandma Emma May, my mother Helen May, and I all have the common middle name of May. Louisa May Alcott, a distant cousin, encouraged the family to continue to use that name. Looking at the Fitch family records, they were obedient to her request. The name, May, appears to belong to males and females alike throughout several generations.

After Grandma came to live with us, she would ride in the front seat of our car when our family made frequent visits west of Bedford to the O'Dell or Novinger's farms. She'd look out across the fields and recall the days when there was an expanse of prairie land and only a few farms. She'd always point out the corner where the old Gilead Church once stood. Losing her short term memory by that time, she'd repeat over and over again, "I wonder if there will be as many changes in the next fifty years as we've had in the last fifty years?"

Still in her wheelchair, Grandma loved to be in her own home during the summer months. Aunt Doris took meals to her; Uncle Herman, Cheryl and Keith, and Janelle looked in on her.

Emma May Fitch O'Dell died on a summer morning in the same room where Grandpa had experienced physical death eight years earlier. When she died on July 1, 1952, she had experienced eighty-five and a half years of changes.

The old farmhouse deteriorated over time and was taken down. I'm glad I still have a faint memory of the house, especially the music of the old mantel clock that sat on a shelf on the west wall of the cozy dining room.

Where's Grandpa?

-A flashback to 1945, written in first person-

"Why are we driving out to the farm so early in the morning, Mama?"

"We have to see my Mama; Papa died last night, Carolyn."

"Tell me what *died* means, Mama."

"It means that the person has left this life, has gone to the next, and we won't see him anymore," Mama said. Her voice is shaky and her lips are quivery. Nothing like this has ever happened before. Mama has never looked so sad and I don't know what to say to her.

"Won't Grandpa come back for my birthday party next week?"

"No, Sweetheart, he won't be coming to your party."

"Will Grandma come to my party?"

"Maybe."

I'm lost in my thoughts for awhile as the old black Ford takes us down the highway, ten miles west of town, to the farm where my Mama grew up. The same farm where her Papa and Mama still live…the same farm where we go to visit every week. A place where I feel loved by Grandpa when I run to his open arms.

I notice that my sister is very quiet. She must be thinking of something to say to Mama. Since Grandma isn't warm and loving like Grandpa, I guess it will be alright if she doesn't come to my party. But I don't know how I can have a party without Grandpa. He has the best bear hugs and scratchy mustache kisses. I know he really loves me.

We are driving up the long driveway to the farmhouse, and I see my grandma standing at the open door. She's saying the same thing over and over, "He loved the children so; he loved the children so." Grandpa would be at that door with his arms open ready to hug me, if he was here. Grandma doesn't hug me. All around me, it feels empty. Grandpa's big cozy rocking chair is still in the corner. Maybe he will come back to it soon and he will let me sit in his lap again, maybe just once more.

My aunts and uncles and cousins are hugging each other. They are speaking with quiet, hushed tones about things like the service, the cemetery, and the music; and all the time Grandma walks from room to room of the old farmhouse saying the same thing, "He loved the children so, he loved the children so."

At the end of the long day, Mama comes into my bedroom to tuck me in.

"Mama, do you think Grandpa is in heaven now?"

"Yes, Honey, I believe he is."

On my knees at the side of the bed, my Mama, my little sister and I go through our nightly routine.

"Can I go first tonight, Mama?"

"Of course, Honey."

> "Now I lay me down to sleep,
> I pray, Dear Lord, my soul to keep.
> Make me loving, kind, and true,
> Make me daily, more like you.
> And give my Grandpa a big hug.
> Amen."

Mother's Club Program

Mama belonged to the Nineteenth Century Club. It always seemed to me like they were about a century too late. Mama liked to talk about the programs, the refreshments, and who the next hostess would be.

When I was trying to put together the dates and times of events in my parents' lives, I found Mom's notes for a talk that she gave at a club meeting sometime in 1989. Like an answered prayer, they fell out of a notebook. Apparently, the topic for the club program that day was something about the changes and differences one had seen during her lifetime. In her familiar writing, on a sheet of white typing paper folded in half, Mom outlined her life. Keeping it just as she wrote it and probably just like she told it, here are her notes for her Nineteenth Century Club:

The Differences Helen Has Seen

I was born on April 30th, 1906. (Showing pictures) I am one year old as I visited country school. When I was two, I had whooping cough. Here is a picture of me when I was three, hugging the hind legs of a horse. When I was four or five years old, I went to Lincoln, Nebraska, and I got my foot caught in a register. It held up the train and the conductor. Here's a picture of the twin ponies that Herman and I rode.

I took piano and organ lessons. I played the (pump) organ at school. These were the numbers I could play by the time I was in 6th or 7th grade:

"America the Beautiful"

"Tenting Tonight"

"Old Kentucky Home"

"Old Black Joe"

"My Country 'Tis of Thee"

"Up on the Housetop"

"One Horse Open Sleigh"

"Battle Hymn of the Republic"

"Silent Night"

"Little Brown Church in the Vale"

After I graduated from country school Herman and I rode horse back or went in a cart to New Market to school, a four mile ride. That was quite a change. Herman was in Junior High and I was a freshman. Clara Mason Cabbage and I were the littlest girls as freshmen. I went to New Market High for two years. I wanted to be a teacher so then I came to Bedford High School for Normal Training. I stayed with Eva Templeton in 1922. She lived across the street from the old locker plant. That was my first experience of living in a Sick Care home. (Eva ran a convalescent home). I was 16. I went home every weekend. Mama was so glad to see me and I was glad to get home.

(Two pictures) Two years of High School went by pretty fast and then I was ready to teach. I was lucky to get the Jones School in 1924-25.

Some of the students were Albert Hensley, Bob and Ross Perkins, Frank Jones, Don Robinson, and one little Churchill girl.

Next year was different. I stayed at home and taught at our home school (Timberlake School) for one year (1925-26). The children wanted to have a program, so we practiced songs and dialogues and made decorations.

Sometimes I'd walk to school and back home in the evenings in the dark, about one and a half to two miles. Sometimes Herman would take me to school then drive to New Market High School.

After teaching two years in country schools, I wanted to go to college, so I could teach in town school. I would have preferred college in Maryville, but at that time, I couldn't teach in Iowa if I graduated from a Missouri school. So I had to go to Cedar Falls to State Teachers College, now called Northern Iowa University. Those were the years 1926, 1927. I chose a two year primary course. I liked every class and teacher the first year. I stayed in the dormitory with a roommate, Helen Walsh.

In the spring of that first year, my mother called to inform me that the neighbors wanted me to teach at the neighborhood school the next year... the Timberlake School. So I decided I could because my bank account was getting small. I taught that year in 1927-28.

Miss Helen O'Dell and college roommate, Helen Walsh, in band uniforms

In November of 1927 I had my first date with Carl.

The next year, 1928-29, I went to college in Cedar Falls again. With Doris (Lucas-O'Dell) as my roommate we stayed with a family who was related to Estel Larison. (Estel later married Doris' sister, Marie). We had fun and it was much different than the first year.

I graduated in the spring of 1929. And the next thing was to get a school. I hoped for one close to home, but didn't get my wish. I took the first school that called me. That was in Brighton, Iowa, which is north of Fairfield. 1929-1930 was a good year. I enjoyed the little youngsters I had teaching kindergarten during first semester and first grade in second semester. One darling little girl has communicated with me at Christmas time every year, until she passed away last December of cancer.

The next year I applied for a teaching job in Villisca and got it. I taught there for four years: 1930-1934.

We were married on July 8, 1934. We took a trip up to Lake Okoboji. On the way home we saw the beautiful grotto in West Bend, Iowa.

We lived two and one and half blocks south of the Court House from July 11 until October 24th. Mrs. Opal Ahrens' mother wanted us to move up to her house on Randolph Street. So we did on October 25, and have lived here ever since.

In 1934, Edith Calhoun asked me to join our Nineteenth Century Club. I did and have been a member for 56 years. Here is my first club book.

On August 29, 1938, Carolyn was born—what a difference she made!

On November 2, 1940, Elaine was born. What a blessing she was!

On January 14, 1948, our dear little boy, Jimmie, was born. We wanted him so much!

Here are our three children and they are grown up and married and have the sweetest and smartest grandchildren, we think, in the world. We have four grandsons and four granddaughters.

We have seen many differences in our lives!

A favorite picture of Mom and Dad. Mom is wearing her favorite color, red. Dad is in his casual blue cardigan. The tulips are in bloom, the grass is green, and "the sky looks like more rain is on the way."

Cousins

Louisa May Alcott, a distant cousin of mine on my mother's side, wrote a novel entitled *Eight Cousins*. I was blessed with an even dozen. Twelve cousins. Ten on my mother's side of the family and two on my father's side.

My mother was one of four children. All of them were born on the O'Dell family farm on Iowa's highway 2, about ten miles west of Bedford. All of her siblings married and had children.

Her oldest brother and family moved to McPaul, Iowa, a tiny town about sixty miles west of Bedford. The others stayed within ten miles of each other. These brothers and sisters, along with the in-laws and children, staged large family gatherings frequently; family dinners, they called them. I don't remember when a family gathering was not centered around food, usually an early afternoon dinner. They rotated the family gatherings among the four homes. Two of them lived on farms, places that offered large yards to play in, horses to ride, haymows to explore, outhouses (before indoor plumbing was installed), a well with a pump, bucket, and long-handled dipper, animals to enjoy, and nature walks in the timber or the pastures. Wide, open spaces.

When we went to Uncle Bruce and Aunt Josephine's home in McPaul, the kids had a separate house with all the game tables that could entertain a family of four sons. From oldest to youngest, they are Bob, Lyndon, Bernard, and Lane O'Dell. Aunt Neva and Uncle Wilbur Novinger lived on a farm about eight miles west of Bedford. Their children: Johnny, Helen, and Louise were like older siblings because of the close and loving relationship between Mom and her sister Aunt Neva. Uncle Herman and Aunt Doris lived on the family farm west of Bedford. Their three children: Cheryl, Keith, and Janelle are exactly the same ages as my siblings and me. Could that have been a coincidence?

During the winter the kids played board games or cards. The girls usually had to segregate themselves at some point and have some serious girl talk and giggling. This was before television, videos, CDs, DVDs, and all other technical contraptions. Sometimes the kids were encouraged to give some kind of performance for the adults. As I remember, we were all well-behaved children!

The women planned the menu, cooked the food, set the table, fed the crowd and cleaned up the dishes and dining room. That seemed to be an unwritten law of the prairie. They always prepared an amazing spread of food. Most of the menus featured a main dish of fried chicken or roasted turkey. Each lady brought her favorite covered dish. Each one had a specialty: homemade yeast bread and rolls, dripping with homemade butter and jam, baked beans (made from scratch), fresh garden vegetables, homemade cakes and pies, and sometimes, a few freezers of home-made ice cream. Sugar found its way into almost everything. Colorful gelatin salads added to the variety of the bountiful buffet.

The men had the job of driving the family to and from the event, and when they arrived, they segregated themselves as far from the kitchen as possible. They told stories and laughed. More stories. More laughter. I think their stories got better each time they were told. Uncle Herman's loud rolling laugh could be heard above the noisy excitement of the crowd of twenty aunts, uncles, and cousins. I recall these large gatherings with fond memories-- some of the happiest days of my childhood.

Before leaving a family gathering, the women would decide when and where the next reunion would be and what foods they would prepare. If Christmas was coming soon, they had the children draw names or make decisions about gift-giving.

These families experienced hardships. There was major flood damage to one home, total loss of another home to fire, a serious car accident, and death of a baby. They were survivors. They were the salt-of-the-earth people. The farmers shared farming machinery and helped each other with the harvesting of crops. They knew how to have fun. Sometimes the adults would play cards. Pitch was the name of their game. The country aunts and uncles would never come to town without a stop off at Uncle Carl's and Aunt Helen's. Even a brief visit from someone in our extended family was a happy occasion.

Six of my country cousins attended the one room school where my mother was a teacher--the same school where my mother attended, along with her siblings, and several of her O'Dell cousins. When our town school in Bedford had a vacation day, Elaine and I would visit the Timberlake School with Keith and Cheryl. We would sometimes walk to the O'Dell farm after school, a distance of about two miles, just like Mom used to do when she was teaching there and lived at home on the O'Dell farm.

In the one room school, the black wood stove sat near the teacher's desk. Student desks of various sizes stood in rows facing the stove. A big upright piano sat along one wall near the stage area. A curtain hung from a wire across the front of the stage. These were the necessary props for the country school programs that I loved to attend. Children from kindergarten through eighth grade all sang together. Students at each grade level gave some kind of performance. Cousin Louise usually gave a reading, a convincing one woman performance depicting more than one person. Some of the older children played the piano. These were big social events for the rural families and children.

There was a one room country school house in every township before school consolidation. After that the children rode to Bedford on the yellow school buses.

Feeling like sisters and brothers, my cousins helped make wonderful memories. I think we were close because our parents stayed connected. Their love for each other trickled down to the next generation. I'm so glad it happened that way.

Additional photos and written articles can be found in a website created by Patricia Combs O'Dell, Keith's wife. It is included here with Pat's permission:

genpat@netins.net

For early photographs of Bedford as well as family photos this website is an amazing collection that Pat has put together:

http://iagenweb.org/taylor/pictures/odell/odell106.jpg

There were only two cousins on my Dad's side of the family, but their boundless energy made up for the smaller number. Dad's only sister, Blanche, married Dale Rankin, and they had two boys, Bill and Ben. They lived in Omaha during most of their lives. But for a week or two each summer, Aunt Blanche and Bill and Ben took the bus from Omaha to Clarinda, where we met them for the drive to Bedford. Their Omaha apartment was small; it seemed like Bill and Ben had stored up their energy all year, eager to be released during their visit to Iowa where they stayed with Grandpa Clyde and Grandma Florence.

Elaine and I experienced daringly different things with our city cousins. We learned about boy stuff. Bill and Ben became reacquainted with their BB guns which stayed at Grandma's house. They taught Elaine and me how to aim and fire. We'd line up cans on fence posts in the barnyard, chicken yard, or pasture, and fire away.

Since the city cousins usually came to Bedford in July, fireworks were plentiful and could be purchased legally. By some miracle, none of us were ever burned or hurt.

Grandma had a chicken yard full of future fryers. Eventually, it was bound to happen; the chickens, the BB guns and the fire crackers all come together in the same chapter.

We were fascinated with the chickens' curiosity, especially around moving objects. We were amazed at the speed that a chicken could hop away from a flying BB as it whizzed by. It was never our intent to actually hit the chicken, but a few tail feathers got clipped in the process. We noticed how chickens swoop into a circle, like folk dancers when food was thrown into the chicken's yard. Naturally we picked up all kinds of objects and threw them into their yard.

Finally, our curiosity caused us to investigate the combination of chickens and firecrackers. A few small firecrackers were thrown into the chicken yard. I won't say who threw them. Unfortunately, one of Grandma's curious chickens met with disaster when it picked up a firecracker at exactly the wrong moment. How in the world did we think we could get away with it? I've blocked this next part from my memory, but I've heard the story many times. The unlucky chicken was left with a dangling beak. As the firecracker went off, so did the beak; well, only part of it. Grandma and Aunt Blanche had to be told. Aunt Blanche was firm with Bill. I suspect she thought our experiment had been his idea. It's never easy being the oldest. She made him kill the chicken by decapitation. It was a struggle for him to do and for us to watch.

It was almost unbearable to look at the platter of fried chicken being passed around Grandma's dinner table later that day. My appetite vanished on the spot.

One afternoon while we four were playing in the upstairs rooms and out on the balcony, Ben and I decided to lock Bill and Elaine out of the house. I don't remember any of the circumstances or what prompted us to lock the east balcony door. Seeing no other way to get downstairs, Bill and Elaine began to climb up and over the steep gables, hoping to find an open window on the flat roof on the other side of the house. Somehow they avoided a long fall from the second story, as they carefully slid down the other side of the gables. Mom heard unfamiliar noises on the roof. She hurried outside to investigate at the same time Bill and Elaine jumped onto the flat roof over the back porch. They were rescued by Mom who unlocked the west window and let them inside, after which she had a little talk with Ben and me.

It's a wonder we didn't cause injury or death. Common sense and experience are good tools. At times, we had neither, but we had fun; daring, boy-stuff fun.

The four of us dug a foxhole on the property line between our house and Grandma's house. We worked all morning. It was large enough for all of us to fit into and become invisible. Then Daddy came home from work, took one look at the hole and said, "Fill it up." Sometimes our bright ideas weren't accepted as such.

My childhood was definitely enriched by the variety of experiences I had with my twelve first cousins.

A few of us have moved away from that area in Iowa where we were raised, but most of the family still lives in the southwest regions of Iowa. Possibly the reason I still call that part of the country "home."

Daddy's Guided Tour

Part 1

For a long time, we three kids had been asking Daddy to record some stories of his childhood. The tape recorder sat beside his favorite recliner, ready for him to talk to it.

A year went by.

No stories had been put on tape, and we made another request. We finally surmised that without an audience, talking into a machine was not very inspiring. So Jim had an idea. He asked Daddy if he would tape stories of his early life as we drove to memorable places. He agreed. In fact, I think he really got a kick out of it. This is how it happened.

One July day in 1996, when I was home in Iowa, Daddy gave us a *guided tour*. Jim drove. I had the back seat all to myself. Daddy occupied the passenger seat with the tape recorder on his lap. He directed Jim, our capable chauffeur, to head south on the St. Joe road and Daddy began speaking to the machine and his audience of two.

Using his practiced oratorical voice, he began with these words:

"I was born in Davis County, northwest of Bloomfield, in a little rural community called Bunch, Iowa." (Earlier Daddy had explained how the town got its name. He said that there was just a bunch of houses there, so it was called Bunch!)

"It is located on the Chicago-Rock Island Railroad, from Chicago to Kansas City; it went right by my Grandpa (Alonzo) Cummings' barn. It was an exciting time for me to see those big, long trains, especially at midnight when the Golden State Limited passenger train was on its way from

Chicago to California, all lit up with lots of activity and a great big rumble as it went by."

Then he told us of his childhood and how he "came to live" in southwestern Iowa. A summary follows:

When Dad was a three year old child, his own father, Clyde E. Cummings began a new career in auctioneering. He boarded a train in Centerville, Iowa, that took him to the Missouri Auctioneer School in Trenton, Missouri. Clyde completed his training within a year and returned to Davis County to work temporarily until he could establish his own area.

The family decided to relocate in southwestern Iowa, near Florence's family.

Until a permanent home and location could be found, the family of three stayed with Florence's sister, Mary and her husband, Pearl Whicker. That was in 1910. Then Clyde set out to find a territory that needed an auctioneer and a new home for his family. He drove a team and buggy down to Sheridan, Missouri, about twelve miles south of Mary and Pearl's farm.

Within a day he had found himself a new community, a few new friends, and a banker who gave Clyde temporary work until his auctioneer business became stable.

My Dad recalled the family's moving day like this:

"On May 11, 1910, we loaded up our furniture which had been moved from Bunch, Iowa, by rail and stored at Uncle Pearl's farm. Two teams and two wagons moved the furniture. As we started down the hill into Sheridan, Missouri, the trees were in full bloom. It was a very impressive sight."

Before reaching Sheridan, Dad pointed out places of interest along the way. The Jones School, just off the St. Joe Road, was where Mama launched her teaching career. Honey Creek came next. Daddy spoke of his long time friend, Frank

Jones, who owns property there. The next point of interest was Forest Grove Cemetery. The cemetery was barely visible from the road. Only a few markers could be seen. Forest Grove Church had been struck by lightning, and it burned to the ground many years ago.

Filling our time along the way, my brother and I requested that Daddy tell about the stunt pilot and airplane at the Taylor County Fair. He always liked telling about the first airplane he ever saw in 1915.

The young female pilot was Ruth Law. Her small plane was dismantled, moved to the fairground, and reassembled there for all to see. The pilot was strapped into a wicker seat that sat in front of the plane's motor. She had all the necessary attire: goggles, cap, gloves, and boots. She lifted off along the back of the racetrack, circled around a few times, and landed the plane back on the track in front of thousands of astonished spectators.

Ruth was in a flying class of eight people. Seven had already met their untimely deaths. She retired soon after her performance at the fairground. She said she wanted to quit while she was still alive!

We drove into Sheridan, Missouri, as though we were traveling down Disneyland's Main Street in a private touring car. Sheridan is an old town, but well preserved. It could be a movie set for a small town in the 1940s. I sat back and enjoyed not only Dad's narrative, but also the remarkable memories that were recalled, as though we were in another time.

The first point of interest was the gymnasium, the only building left on the school ground. Daddy watched the school being built in 1914 and remembered having his picture taken beside the gym in 1918.

Not wanting to omit some of the distinctive voice of my Dad, I will try to include a word for word account of a portion of our journey through the town.

"Sheridan had more sidewalks than any little town around. My Dad had a sidewalk block in the park with his name on it: *C.E. Cummings, Auctioneer.*

"There were produce houses, businesses, and grocery stores here; the buildings on the East have been taken away. Oh, here's the city well! It's the city waterworks now. The well was never pumped dry. There used to be a water tank there where people watered their horses.

"On the south side of the street were more business houses. The old hotel sat clear to the East. It's gone now. There was a harness shop on the North side. This is the bank building where Wally Sanders worked. It's a Post Office now. I think the drug store is gone. Claude Sharp ran the drug store.

"Turn to the right, and we'll go west up Main Street. Here was the bank; it's moved to Grant City (Missouri) now. Here was Spalding's Meat Market. They didn't have any refrigeration, but they brought their meat in and butchered it, and you bought your meat while it was still *fresh.*"

Dad remembered names of people, the business each one owned, and where it was located. The men's clothing store, the grocery store, the Christian Church, where his family attended church came next. Decades later Daddy preached the one hundredth anniversary of that church.

There was a hitching rack around the park (only a portion remains today). Dad pointed out the home of his best buddy, Neil Naill. Neil's house had a real bathrub, a novelty at that time. We saw the hardware store, Doc Nesbitt's office, and the home of his Sunday School teacher, Miss Streeter. We drove by the little lavender-colored house where Dad and his parents lived for eight years. This was the house where his little sister, Blanche, was born.

Grandma Florence and Carl, age five, on the porch of the lavender-colored house in Sheridan, Missouri

Jim and I asked Dad to tell us about the tragic death of his best friend, Neil. We had heard the story before, but hearing it again, in this town, let us sense it more completely. When Neil was ten years old, he drowned in a pond while his family was picnicking with friends. Another ten year old friend, Harry Longfellow and Daddy were the honorary pallbearers at Neil's funeral. The church bells tolled at the Methodist Church as the little procession walked to the cemetery. Daddy and Harry walked ahead of the procession. It made a lasting impression on ten year old Carl Cummings.

We saw the burial place of Neil as Daddy continued to tell stories of their close friendship. They lived across the alley, and they stayed with each other almost every night. Daddy stayed at Neil's the night that Blanche was born in 1915. The next morning Mrs. Naill told eight year old Carl that there was a surprise at his house. She took him home to see the new member of the family. "I had no idea," he said.

Neil Naill and Carl Cummings
Easter Sunday, April 23, 1916
They are both eight years old.

Before leaving Sheridan, we crossed the Platte River and saw the location of the old grist mill and the barn where Daddy's family kept their old *drivin'* horse and buggy. The same buggy shed was used for the family's first automobile, a 1916 Overland. We saw the sliding hill where Daddy and his friends poured water at night so they could slide down the frozen hill the next day.

It seemed like I was on the front row of a live version of *Our Town*. With his remarkable memory, Daddy recalled the names of people in his past and events that happened there, events that shaped his life.

Part 2

We left Worth County, the smallest county in Missouri, and entered Nodaway County on our way to Hopkins, Missouri. Grandma Florence was born in Hopkins, so Daddy decided that our guided tour needed to include the Hopkins Cemetery so that all of his ancestors would be mentioned on the audio tape. So we headed west to Hopkins.

The Brethern Cemetery and Church were mentioned as we passed the spot where they once stood. As a boy Daddy remembered going to the Brethern Church once a year where they had a basket dinner after which a foot washing was done...on one foot only!

Daddy called off the names of owners of each farm, the number of acres of each, and a story about most of them. Jim and Daddy agreed that the crops of corn along the road were better than "waist high by the fourth of July."

Daddy remembered the big celebration held in Sheridan at the end of World War I on November 11, 1918. At 4:00 AM the train whistle blew incessantly. The depot agent received a telegraph that the war was over. The hardware stores sold out of shells. Guns were fired into the air. Sheridan was alive with excitement!

The following spring, on March 1st, 1919, Daddy's family moved from Sheridan, Missouri, to Bedford, Iowa. Grandpa Clyde wanted to widen his territory in the auctioneer business to include Bedford. He had already secured the Sheridan and Hopkins areas. Grandpa knew that he could make a living by combining farming with the auctioneer business.

Trains were used to get around from town to town; so when Grandpa Clyde went to Bedford for any kind of business, it took him two days. The first day of the trip was a Great Western train ride north to Diagonal, Iowa. After an overnight stay in a hotel, he caught the H&S at about 4 A.M.

and went to Burlington Junction. About 7 P.M. he caught the CB&Q that ran from Creston to Bedford. Eighteen miles in two days!

For two seasons (1919 and 1920) Clyde and Florence farmed on Grandpa Herbert's farm southwest of Bedford. This allowed Grandpa to "make a living" while commencing the auctioneer business in Bedford. Their move into Bedford was made in the fall of 1920, the year that Aunt Blanche started into kindergarten and Daddy started into eighth grade. They lived in a little house on King Street from September until March, later moving to a house on Jackson Street where they lived until 1928, the year they moved up on the hill on Randolph Street.

While attending Auctioneer School in Trenton, Missouri, Clyde met Ivan Wells, who later became a neighbor and partner at the sale barn. After they graduated, Ivan, who was eighteen years old, took the New Market (Iowa) territory, his home town. Ivan stayed in Bedford with Clyde and Florence, paying board and room during the week and going home to New Market on the weekends. When he married Esta, they moved to the house on the north end of Randolph Street. Later, on March 1st, 1928, Clyde and Florence moved to the first house south of Ivan and Esta on Randolph Street.

In 1921 Ivan began the Bedford Sales at the Sale Barn on east Main Street, a business that thrived in Bedford until 1994. There was a sale every Saturday in the Sale Barn where one could hear Clyde and Ivan shouting out the auctioneers' cry as farmers brought their cattle and pigs to market. There were no scales at the time for weighing the animals, so they were sold by the head. Grandpa Clyde was training young Carl to take over the auctioneer business someday. He would ask him to estimate the weight of an animal, the only way to determine what it was worth. After learning the auctioneers' cry, Daddy practiced his new skill as he auctioned off lunch boxes at the country schools' socials.

While we drove on to Hopkins, Daddy filled the time with stories of his job as a gas station attendant. His last two years of high school, he worked for one dollar a day at the Standard Oil Company station, which sat on the corner where the State Savings Bank is today. He remembered that some families in Bedford tried to live on one dollar a day in the early 1920's. There were only two gas stations in Bedford then. The other was a Sinclair station where the City Hall stands today. Gas cost twelve cents a gallon, and a quarter would buy a whole quart of oil!

With no gas gauges in the cars, the measurement was taken by inserting a ruler or stick into the gas tank. The tank was located under the front seat of the car.

Dad worked all day on Saturdays or Sundays, much of the time sitting at the desk looking out the front window. When the station was taken down, Dad's sentimental side got the best of him, and he asked if he could have that front window and frame. It was reused in the house at 608 Randolph Street many years later when the front porch was removed and the upstairs door was changed into a window! How's that for recycling?

Dad had planned to continue working at the station after high school graduation where he and Albert Salen had agreed to split the grand sum of one hundred and fifty dollars each month. Each of them would work half a day, thereby giving them half of each day to embark on another endeavor. Dad thought at the time that it seemed like a winning situation.

Then one day W. E. Crum, Jr. stopped by to visit with Dad in the oil station. He offered Dad an opportunity to work in the Bedford National Bank as bookkeeper. His salary at first was sixty-five dollars a month. Daddy began working at the BNB on June 15, 1925, as bookkeeper. Forty-five years later, as Executive Vice President, Dad retired from the bank.

Dad concluded with this thought: "The banking business has changed like everything else. I thought at one time I knew how to run a bank, but today I wouldn't know anything about it."

Part 3

We arrived in Hopkins, Missouri.

Daddy began with some history of the Herbert family.

Dad's mother, Florence Herbert Cummings, was born on October 12, 1881, in Hopkins, Missouri. We drove down the street where the house once stood. When she was five years old, her family homesteaded in Kansas. They tried to grow corn but found that the corn crops could not stand up to the dry winds of Kansas, so Grandma Florence's parents returned to Hopkins, Missouri.

Our next stop was the Hopkins Cemetery north of the small town. We visited graves of Matilda and Isaac Herbert, parents of Grandma Florence.

Isaac's parents, Jesse and Martha, or Patsy as she was called, were buried nearby. Traditionally, Grandma Florence and Dad would drive to Hopkins each year on Memorial Day and decorate these graves. Jesse Herbert was a circuit rider, and his last charge was the Methodist Church in Hopkins.

Norris Herbert, a brother of Isaac, was a Civil War veteran who survived imprisonment at Andersonville. He was shot in the leg. Had it not been for the stream of fresh water that suddenly appeared at one end of the prison grounds, he might not have been able to keep the wound clean and save his leg. The 30,000 Union soldiers barely survived on cornmeal in a space hardly large enough for 10,000 prisoners.

Dad's Uncle Roy, brother of Grandma Florence, often told Daddy that he was the "spittin' image" in size and stature of Uncle Norris Herbert! Dad remembered meeting Uncle Norris, the veteran hero of the family.

Leaving the Hopkins Cemetery we traveled north on Highway 148. Shortly after crossing the Iowa/Missouri state line, we approached the area of the former Hazel Dell community and turned left off of the highway. There is now a house where the little one room Hazel Dell schoolhouse once stood. The school has now been moved to the top of the hill.

"Uncle Roy's farm was on the right side. My cousin, Gladys Herbert Marsh (daughter of Roy and Bell Herbert) attended Hazel Dell School, Ross #9. I remember attending Christmas programs at the one room school. Gas lanterns lit up the room. Large crowds of parents and families attended the programs.

"My Dad (Clyde) helped to take down the little Hazel Dell Baptist church, and the lumber was reused to build the Baptist parsonage beside the Baptist Church in Bedford," recalled Daddy.

We took a left turn at the top of the hill.

"Great Grandpa Jesse Herbert's house was just to the south of the corner."

It had been reduced to a pile of rubble.

Daddy continued, "I remember a letter that he wrote in 1892 telling of the times he would look down into the 102 River Valley when the train came through and listen to that whistle that echoed and re-echoed throughout the valley.

"Jesse Herbert passed away in the house that once stood on this site. He lived to be sixty years old. He was buried down in Hopkins, because Hopkins was their trading post with the church where he last preached.

"After he died, Great Grandma Patsy lived with Matilda, her daughter, until her death. They lived about six or seven miles straight north of where we are now. Great Grandma Patsy broke her hip and never walked after that so she was a wheel chair person. She is buried beside her husband in Hopkins.

"My Grandmother Townsend and her husband, William Townsend, my Grandmother Herbert's parents, are buried in Graceland Cemetery. That was the closest cemetery to where Grandpa Herbert lived, and in the horse and buggy days, you went to the closest cemetery. My Great Grandmother Townsend, who lived at Grandpa Herbert's, passed away in June before I was born in July (1907). Grandma Herbert came back to Davis County and was with my mother when I was born.

"We lived on eighty acres in Davis County (Iowa). We lived there until we moved to Sheridan (Missouri).

"Grandpa Cummings (Alonzo) bought me a little rocking chair when I was just three years old. I suppose they got it at Sears and Roebuck, because we went down to the depot and brought it home in a little crate. I remember unwrapping it, and I've had it eighty-six years. It's in the south bedroom with the antiques in the house at *608 Randolph Street."*

We traveled west on the Golden Rod road, past Ferris and Patsy Gray's house.

"Coming up is the Ross #3 School (Patch School) where I went to country school. My teacher was Georgie Parker Miller's sister, Lois. She was a very, very good teacher. I wouldn't take anything for my two years in country school (grades 6 and 7). I'd ride my pony to school. I'd put my lunch in one pocket and two ears of corn for the pony in the other pocket. When it was bad and I couldn't ride the pony, I'd walk across the field. This pond was our skating rink in the wintertime. At one time there were twenty-five children going to this school."

Daddy explained how his father Clyde raised hogs on the ten acres and had to carry water from the house. We saw the location of Grandpa Herbert's farm, the corner where the house sat, the good *coastin'* hill in the winter, where the row of oak trees grew west of the house, and the fields where oats were grown. The 102 River is just to the west of the farm.

We continued on the country roads as Dad's amazing memory took him back to another time. He pointed out locations of farms of several people, who used to live there, who bought and sold, the number of acres in each farm, and who lives there now. When we got to the Ray Dawson farm, Dad remembered that he worked there one summer for a dollar a day. That was before his job at the Standard Oil Station.

Driving into the iron archway of the little country cemetery called Graceland, Dad began to rattle off family lineage. On his side of the family, he named his Grandparents Herbert's parents, the Townsends (William and Christina Boyer Townsend). On my mother's side of the family are graves of Jabez Fitch, Lyman Fitch, Ashley Fitch and wife, Mary; Hugh Fitch and wife, Esther, of Leonia, New Jersey; May Fitch O'Dell and Lester O'Dell, and their son, Herman O'Dell.

Daddy continued to talk to the recorder as Jim and I got out of the car and walked among the ancestors' gravesites.

"The little cemetery is mowed up nice and neat. The township maintains it with taxation. It will always be here and taken care of."

Recalling the way of life of these early prairie people, Dad summed it up like this:

"Most of the families were large families. They lived on the farm and made their living from the soil. If a family bought and paid for a farm in their lifetime, it was an accomplishment. The farm life, as I knew it, when I was a lad, was a good way of life. We milked cows, separated the cream and gave the skimmed milk to the pigs. We made cottage cheese. We had chickens that laid eggs. We had our own meat from butchering our hogs; we cured our own meat. I'd still like to have a serving of home-cured ham and eggs, a "purty" good kind of a diet, a little heavy on the fat and grease. I've lived to be eighty-nine years old this month, and Helen is ninety. That was our diet. We ate a lot of bread and gravy. We raised a lot of potatoes and canned everything from the garden that we could find. We had apples and potatoes in bins and caves. No refrigeration and electricity. The farm life was a good kind of life. The folks knew where we were. We had chores to do after school. It was a fun time in the winter; we'd go coasting.

"I had a dog named Bounce because when he'd run, he just bounced from one jump to the other. When we had a fresh snow, I'd take Bounce outside, and in just a little while, we'd catch a few rabbits. In the snow they couldn't get away from Bounce. We'd skin them and dress them and hang them on the clothesline to freeze because we didn't have refrigeration. There must have been a lot of vitamins in those rabbit legs. We seemed to thrive on them. I'd still like to have a good ol' rabbit leg."

Our guided tour ended with Daddy's recording of the auctioneer cry. I'd been asking him to record that all day!

After his auctioneer's cry had ended, he concluded our two hour journey with these words, "It's been nice to visit with 'ya," he said into the recorder, " and blessings on 'ya."

Thanks to Jim's idea and Daddy's remarkable memory, the recording of that tour can be listened to again and again.

The tape is a keeper.

Chapter Five

Early Memories

On Daddy's Knees

We'd catch him in his big brown chair. After a full day of working at the bank, then tending to the farm chores at the barn, Daddy would go to his chair and wait until Mom had finished preparing dinner. We'd watch and wait for him to transform his image from the businessman's white shirt and tie into the comfortable loose-fitting Lee's bib overalls. His big overstuffed chair sat in the corner of the living room beside the General Electric radio, housed inside a tall wooden cabinet, large enough for a doily and vase on top. I'm sure Daddy wanted to read the daily paper, listen to the news, and relax. But Elaine and I had other ideas for this time. This was our time to play with Daddy. We each straddled one of Daddy's knees. Then he'd bounce us on his knees and sing the "To-Dat" song:

"To-Dat, To-Dat, To-Dat, To-Dat." He'd sing this intro until we were ready.

"Two little girls on the way to school
Spied a fish in a brook so cool.
One had a line
One had a hook
One had a bee in a reading book.
To-Dat, To-Dat, To-Dat, To-Dat."

"Again, Daddy, sing it again," we'd say.

He lifted alternate knees with each To-Dat, the faster the better! Elaine and I loved the challenge of staying on. Sometimes the To-Dats would cause us to gently roll off, like a saddle slipping quietly over the side of a horse. We'd laugh and ask for a repeat performance. Kids like repetition.

We'd also request a game of hide the ring. Daddy's bib overalls provided numerous places for him to hide his ring while Elaine and I closed our eyes. He'd tell us when to open them, and we'd start unsnapping the various compartments until one of us found his gold ring. Occasionally, Daddy would place the ring behind one of his ears, a place we seldom thought to look.

Daddy often said that Mom would have his two little girls looking as *cute as a bug's ear* when he came home for lunch. However cute that is, I couldn't say, but it was a favorite expression of Daddy's. Mom made us matching dresses until we were tired of looking like the Bobbsey twins. She'd buy material and sew for a couple of days and turn out original outfits for Elaine and me. She finished the clothes with handmade buttonholes because her old treadle machine didn't have an automatic buttonhole attachment. Mom made all of our clothes with *lots of love* until we were about eight and ten years old. At that age we didn't feel as cute as a bug's ear wearing matching dresses. I can still remember the shopping trip to Thompson's Mercantile when Elaine and I got to pick out our own unique and unmatched dresses.

While sitting on Daddy's lap, he would let us watch him roll his own cigarettes. The brown, poignant-smelling, zippered pouch would be brought out, along with the thin cigarette papers. We thought the delicate job of placing the narrow row of tobacco in just the right place and exactly down the middle of the paper was a clever accomplishment. Finally, with a quick lick along the long edge, he would roll up the cigarette and place it on the nearby ashtray ready to be lit. Daddy quit smoking, cold turkey, when Jim was born. Later he told me that he never wanted his son to see him smoke. Daughters just couldn't capture that place of importance and pride like a male child could. I don't remember when I first realized that. But that's okay; after all, the folks waited a long time for Jimmie!

I'm sure that Daddy bounced Jim on his knee and sang the "To Dat" song to him, too, but I don't remember. By that time I had about all I could do just trying to be a *cool* adolescent.

Bibbins Park

The end of a sultry summer day would often be topped off with a ride to Bibbins Park. It was a place of entertainment for kids of all ages, in the midst of a forest of towering oaks and maples and pine trees.

The short ride across town in our car cooled us off. An air-conditioned car in those days was a car with opened windows going at a speed of twenty-five miles per hour. However, this type of air-conditioning had limitations; it did not suck the humidity out of the air.

The heavy, black gate at the park entrance was seldom closed. The trees formed an umbrella over the playground area like a mother hen protecting her chicks. My sister and I were never allowed out of the car until Mama had slathered us with citronella. This was a pungent liquid that came in a dark, little bottle, whose contents never ran dry.

We raced to the dangerously high slide, squealing all the way down. Then we made ourselves dizzy on the self-propelled merry-go-round. Sometimes we'd try jumping off as it was still whirling at top speed. This proved disastrous many times. We balanced our weight on each end of the teeter totter. It was more fun to be on the high end of the ride. We'd enlist Mom's energy to push us in the swings. Sometimes, she'd swing, too.

The trees were full of ticks, and the night air was filled with mosquitoes. Old style 1940s street lamps lit up the playground so that we seldom thought of the dark wooded areas around the playground. The little dirt road twisted around the trees and crossed a tiny creek below. The tennis courts were similarly lit for night playing. Most of the time the park was our private acre of childhood memories.

In the 1920s a pharmacist, Mr. A.L. Bibbins, left money for the city of Bedford to build a park. I'm glad he did.

Back home, after each romp at the park, Mama would check our ears, necks and legs for ticks. Then we'd climb into the big tub for a warm bubble bath. We'd try to neutralize the strong aroma of the citronella.

The scent of citronella still takes me back to carefree evenings at Bibbins Park at the end of a hot summer day in Iowa.

Mama Liked Curls

Mama seemed drawn to children, especially those with curly hair.

I'm mighty thankful that little brother Jim's hair took on a few wavy directions, since Elaine and I had ramrod straight hair. Jim's comment about his hair doing *back bends* was one of Mama's favorite lines that she remembered and repeated often. That's okay. The folks waited a long time for Jimmie!

Mama set out to fix the fact of nature that her little girls did not have curls. She would often say, "Oh, look at that cute little curly-headed kid." I was starting to think that there could be no cuteness without curls. So Elaine and I went along with her wishes for us to have curly hair. She tried many methods on us. Some of those methods were most unpleasant; some a little less painful and annoying than others. This is what I remember.

The first curlers Mama used on our hair were metal rollers. She'd roll up our freshly washed hair with the rollers, vertically positioned around our heads. We wore them until our hair dried. These made long bouncy curls that lasted for a couple of days, if we were lucky.

Rags were easier to sleep on. This method required a strip of cloth which Mama would use to wrap our long hair around and around. Then the two ends of the cloth were knotted together. We tried not to sleep on the knots. We looked like something from outer space, but the result was what Mama wanted. Lots and lots of curls. Cute little curly-headed kids.

Mama liked to use a setting gel called Wave Set. It was a thick, green, sticky, slimy goo, and it came in a glass jar. It really did *set* the hair. Mama was good at setting hair. She set hair for several ladies, right in our own kitchen. She could have had her own beauty shop. Finger waves were the style for older women. Grandma Florence washed her own hair every Saturday before she came to our house for her *finger wave set*. Mama used a ton of Wave Set as she coaxed the hair to bend into waves before affixing it with a metal pincher-type clamp. When the hair was dry, it was stiff and unmovable. A strong wind might blow through town and literally take branches off a tree, but not a hair would be disturbed if it had been glued down with Wave Set.

Whenever women needed longer lasting curls and *body,* they paid a lot of money for a hot wave permanent at the beauty shop. Elaine and I did not manage to escape this type of torture. We'd sit on the riser board placed across the arms of the beauty shop chair. Our hair was wound onto rods. That wasn't the bad part. After our heads were covered with rods, we'd endure the dreaded hot clamps, which were snapped over every rod. The clamps dangled at the end of the electric wires that originated under a giant hood. When every hair was wound up and clamped down, the beauty operator (alias executioner) turned on the heat. Sometimes a clamp would be too close to the skin leaving a scalp or neck burn. Or we would feel the pull of a clump of hair wound too tightly around a rod. It seemed like we had no choice but to endure the pain and hope for the time to pass as quickly as possible.

How we loved the welcomed words, "All done. Time's up." Then the hot clamps were removed, and the hair was unwound from the rods. I was usually mortified at the mound of tight curls on my head. But Mom liked her "cute, little curly-headed girls" and the worst part was when she'd stand us up in front of her old Kodak camera and take a photograph of us entitled *new permanents*. Sometimes I'd wear a hat or scarf until the curls settled down.

Then, in the 50s, a new improved permanent wave became popular. It was called the *cold wave* permanent or the home permanent. Some of the brand names were **Toni** and **Lilt.**

Mom liked these better, but they weren't much better for a kid. There were stinky neutralizers and liquid fixatives that had to be saturated on every strand of hair. Strong ammonia smells caused a kid to come up gasping for fresh air. The rods were plastic and light weight and could be re-used. Mama's set of plastic rods were loaned out and used over and over by many friends and neighbors.

One time Mom decided it might be a smart idea to sanitize the little plastic rods. So she dumped them into a large kettle of boiling water and left them for a while to sanitize. Lifting the lid of the kettle later, she peered in and shouted, "Why, forevermore." Those once-straight plastic rods were bent, twisted and curled in every direction! When I think of that pot of curly plastic curlers, I still have to laugh.

The popular magazine and television commercial posed the question: "Which twin has the Toni?" Of course, both identical twins had the same soft, natural looking, wavy, identical curls, in the picture. What WAS their secret? My hair never survived the ordeal of a permanent very well and usually came out looking frizzy, fuzzy and fried.

The big question after a permanent was, "Did it take?" Good grief! Did it take? The question should have been, "How long **will** it take before the hair returns to normal?" It usually took several months before my hair recovered from a home permanent.

Liberation time was when I learned how to make pin curls using bobby pins. I was in junior high, and wasn't the only girl that liked to experiment with hair styles, and learn how to manage her own hair. I was always very particular about the appearance of my hair. Walking around looking like I'd just jumped out of an electric chair was not my idea of fun. So I saved myself from any more permanent miseries and humiliation.

I haven't had a permanent in decades.

I can't imagine, in my wildest dreams, why I would ever have one again. As I get older, my hair performs more *back bends* all by itself.

One summer, not long ago, Elaine and I visited the Taylor County Museum in Bedford. There in a booth was a recreation of the old fashioned beauty shop, and in the corner sat the *monster,* the big hood with electric wires and clamps dangling beneath it. As I remember, we hissed at it, turned away, and I heard Elaine mutter something under her breath. Some things should never have been invented and that was one of them!

Of course, blow dryers and hair color solutions are a part of my life now. But as an adult I get to decide how much work and inconvenience I want to put myself through just to have decent hair.

I take it all in stride!

Life around the Piano

"Mairsy Doats and Dozy Doats and liddle llamzy divey, A kiddley divey too, wouldn't you?"

We would belt it out as we stood around the upright, while Mom's hands moved quickly over the eighty-eight keys. Our neighbors, Bobby Miller and Ruth and Katherine Johnson, joined us around the piano. Bobby played clarinet. Ruth and Katherine sang. Elaine and I, being the youngest, imitated the older kids.

Sometimes Daddy would tune up his old, dented, silver baritone and play along or he might add his strong voice to the group. Later, Cousin Helen sometimes added her clarinet tones while Cousin Louise completed our band with the chiming sounds of the glockenspiel. We loved these melodies with words of hope:

"Coming in on a Wing and a Prayer"

"There'll be Bluebirds over the White Cliffs of Dover"

"When the Lights Go on Again, All over the World"

"Harbor Lights"

"God Bless America" made popular by Kate Smith.

"Praise the Lord and Pass the Ammunition"

"I'll be Seeing You"

The titles of the tunes revealed the times in which we lived. We were waiting and hoping for the war to end. We didn't have to go out to find entertainment; we entertained ourselves at home. Of course, we didn't have much money or enough ration books for gas to take us very far, anyway.

The stack of old sheet music, found in the tall walnut bookcase, brought back memories of that time almost sixty years ago. Marked with Pearly Blake's stamp *Blake Music, Bedford, Iowa*, most of the old music cost fifty cents or less back in the 1940s. What a bargain! I wonder if other households had as much fun with sheet music and singing around the piano.

Pictures of young stars like Bing Crosby and Rudy Valle graced the covers of the sheet music. Titles like these had worn and yellowed covers:

"I Found a Million Dollar Baby in a Five and Ten Cent Store"

"I Love Those Dear Hearts and Gentle People Who Live in my Home town"

"Tip Toe through the Tulips"

"Get Out and Get Under the Moon"

"Just an Echo in the Valley"

No one in town belonged to more clubs than Mom. When she was in charge of the program, Elaine and I were usually the entertainment. Mom would teach us the words and melody to appropriate numbers. Our repertoire grew as we did. The night before the performance, Mom would do up our hair in curlers or rags so that we'd have curls. She'd put us in matching dresses that she had designed and made. Then she would stand us up in front of a group of club ladies or church ladies or service club members or even dinner guests at our house. We loved to sing. Mom did a fine job of playing the piano accompaniment. These were some of our numbers:

"Brighten the Corner"

"Sing and Smile and Pray"

"Jesus Wants Me for a Sunbeam"

"The Wedding of Jack and Jill"

And the usual collection of Christmas numbers.

This was before the electric magnification of sound, so we were always encouraged to sing out loudly and enunciate clearly to be heard. Elaine and I sang our way through high school, still doing duets, but without the curls and matching dresses. There was one exception. In a high school talent show, we did a song and dance routine to "Sisters," a number made popular in the 1954 movie *White Christmas*. We stood in for Rosemary Clooney and Vera Ellen! For that performance we once again had matching blue taffeta dresses, designed and made by Mom.

Not only did we get lots of practice with vocal duets, we played lots of trumpet and piano duets. Sometimes the music teacher at school would ask us to perform for a meeting. We'd be excused from school to make an appearance at an afternoon club or meeting somewhere in town.

Music was and always has been a huge and important part of our lives. The seeds were planted early. I appreciate the cost of lessons, music, instruments, and costumes that the folks laid out for us. But mostly I appreciate the patience they had while listening to "Humoresque" on the piano fifty-six times a day. They never complained about the high, piercing notes of a trumpet, either.

Even to the dying end, Daddy took Elaine and me to various cemeteries with him. He gave the Memorial Day addres, and we played the taps and the echo. One of us would wander off through the headstones to the far end of the cemetery to play the distant echo. We played taps at the Bedford cemeteries, Graceland Cemetery and several other small country cemeteries that dot the countryside of southwest Iowa.

Where are these music makers now?

The old upright piano has been moved to granddaughter Carla's home in Missouri Valley, Iowa. The old dented silver baritone was the only thing that my son Steve wanted from Grandpa's house. It has found a new home in his music studio in Long Beach, California. The two gold cornets that Elaine and I played have been passed through families to young and promising musicians. Mine found its way back to me after making the circuit. The old sheet music has been divided among many of us. Some of it has been framed and hangs on the walls of my home. I still like to sit down and play some of the old tunes on the piano. They don't write 'em like that anymore! I can't play 'em like I used to, either, but I have fun trying.

Many old Etude books and ancient hymnals were found in the tall walnut bookcase. They were divided among our family. The many copies of piano duets are keepers. Elaine and I still have fun trying to play them, and just like we were kids again, we laugh through every number.

With the talent showing up in the grandchildren and great grandchildren, I think that music will have a special place of honor in our family for many generations. I can't imagine a world without music.

Music, Music and More Music

The Victrola

The old Victrola stood the trip quite well from a basement storage room in Aunt Blanche's Omaha apartment to our dining room. Daddy and Mom couldn't allow this great old music machine to be destroyed, and we didn't have a record player at the time. The cherry wood cabinet still had a high gloss. The pungent aroma of the maroon velvet lining inside told of its years in a dark storage area. It was a well-preserved antique. The cabinet with its shallow, horizontal shelves housed many 78 rpm records. The records were heavy and thick, some with cracks and chips. These represented the music of the Gay Nineties and early 1900s. One label was **RCA Victor, His Master's Voice.** It was complete with a picture of the little dog with his head cocked to one side, listening to His Master's Voice coming from the bell of an old Victrola.

The old Victrola had a crank on the right side. We'd wind it up so it could play an entire record before slowing down. "Wang Wang Blues," "How're You Gonna Keep 'em Down on the Farm," "Wabash Blues," "Profiteering Blues," "Missouri Waltz," and a few Sousa marches were played often.

We played those old 78s so many times we had memorized every word and note. A favorite game was our own version of *Name That Tune* in three notes or less. We laughed at the silly lyrics, and we strained to hear the singer's voice, which sounded like someone yelling through a tunnel. Singing into a megaphone produced an echoing kind of sound that Rudy Valle made popular.

We gained a true picture of our grandparents'and parents'music and the songs of their worlds...what made them laugh and cry.

"Climb upon My Knee, Sonny Boy" was sung by Al Jolson with all the drama of a grieving father. Those words would always get to us. We imitated the slide trombone player when we listened to the *blues* and marched around the room as we played the ever popular Sousa Marches. We learned to ignore the sandpaper quality and cracks in the records. We gave those old 78s a second life, a second time around and around and around.

Piano Lessons

My first piano teacher was my mother. She showed me where Middle C was on the keyboard and on the page of music. My first piece was "Indians" and it taught me three notes. I can still play it! So can Elaine and Jim! I remember the words, too. A big effort was made to point out the reason for numbers beside each note. That was the *fingering.* After I learned to play several pieces, Mom thought that I was playing by numbers, not notes, and she let me know that that just wasn't done. She was very disappointed in me. Then she told Daddy when he came home from work. I felt like a failure. Elaine, who was probably about four years old, sat back and took all of this in. She knew what NOT to do and even knew how the pieces should sound. Her learning curve was shorter than mine! It's not easy being the oldest! Elaine developed an ear for music...a real gift.

Mom decided that we needed to have a piano teacher, other than herself. Her first idea was to call upon a young lady named Betty Pote. The Potes, of the Drug store fame, lived on Main Street about two blocks east of Randolph Street. One day Mom sent us to Betty's.

We weren't tall enough to reach the doorbell near the front door. We figured out how to stand on the porch railing and stretch. Betty seemed surprised at our request but agreed to start our lessons. I was about seven years old. Elaine was five.

We had several other piano teachers through the years: Kay Sawyer, Martha Dinwiddie, and Mildred Stacy. Mildred believed there was value in memorizing every piece. She started Elaine and me on piano duets, which would usually be the last thing on the program at her piano recitals. She showed us where she hid the key to the Hammond Organ at the Methodist Church and explained that since she had taught herself to play it, we could do the same. We both helped out with church services at the Methodist Church, as well as the Baptist Church, during our junior high and high school years.

Elaine and I were following in our mother's footsteps when we played for church. Mom had been the pianist for the Methodist Church before the organ was purchased. She would sit in the front near the piano during the services, while Daddy entertained Elaine and me with his drawings of the three bears riding in a convertible! Kids like repetition. That's good, because bears in a convertible were the only things that Daddy could draw!

Jim had piano lessons, also. In addition to the piano, he had an electric keyboard and his own band! **The Rising Sons** had their start on the road to fame in the living room at 608 Randolph. **The Rising Sons** had gigs throughout southwest Iowa. Later, Jim added a portable electric organ to his collection of musical instruments, as well as a trumpet which he played in the high school band.

Music lessons were a good investment. They pay handsome dividends. I hear that **The Rising Sons** still make a rare appearance around the area--dividends still paying off!

There Was a War Going On

It did seem strange that Daddy had to go all the way to Des Moines for a physical, and it seemed strange that he got on the big bus parked at the corner of Main and Court Streets. A large number of men got on the bus, too. Wives were kissing their husbands good-bye. It did seem strange that they would do that if the daddies and husbands of our town were just going for a physical. Mama seemed very sober and quiet. She seemed fragile, too. That wasn't like Mama.

What I didn't know that day was that Daddy did not expect to come back for a very long time. He had taken out life insurance policies for all of us.

After the bus pulled away from the downtown corner, we went back home. The rest of the day Mama kept very busy, doing some of her usual jobs twice. Her answers to our questions weren't really answers at all. It was not a normal day. It was the early spring of 1944 and the world was anything but normal. There was a war going on, and the Allies were preparing for D Day.

That seemed like the longest day in my life. Things were different all day. Daddy didn't come home for lunch. Grandma Cummings came over more times than usual. In my five year old way of thinking, it was a very strange day.

Then the 6:00 P.M. town whistle blew, and Mom rushed Elaine and me to the car. We drove downtown. We anxiously waited at the corner of Main and Court Streets watching for the big Trailways bus to appear. There were just a few others waiting with us.

The bus pulled up to the corner beside Thompson's Mercantile store. The door opened. Several moments later, Daddy and only one other gentleman stepped out of the bus. Mama seemed relieved, sober, and quiet. And she seemed fragile. That wasn't like Mama. Daddy's voice was quiet. I overheard them talking about the word "rejected," whatever that meant. Daddy explained that he couldn't pass the physical because of an accident that took part of his fingers on his left hand. He wouldn't be able to handle a gun, the examiners said. That's the one word that I remember most about that entire day. **Gun.** This was a very different kind of day. Some new thoughts and feelings entered my sheltered, comfortable life, and I suddenly felt older than five years old.

When we got home Daddy reached into his pocket and pulled out two Baby Ruth candy bars, gifts for Elaine and me.

Daddy knew that he might have some physical limitations because of the accident he had had with the electric saw several years before. But losing part of his fingers on his left hand never stopped him from using a typewriter or doing just about anything, for that matter. Daddy thought that perhaps a clerical position would be one way he could serve his country.

But he was rejected. So my Daddy didn't go to war. I wondered how anyone could be away from their daddy for months, maybe years.

We had periodic blackouts in Bedford. Daddy was a block captain. He would put on his trench coat and the black armband over one sleeve and disappear into the night. His was a job carried out by many other volunteer captains about Bedford, each walking door to door in their assigned blocks. He carried a whistle around his neck and used it as he approached each house. Daddy knocked on doors and requested that the occupants cover their windows or turn off their lights for a period of time. We didn't have blackout curtains hanging at our windows. Mama would tape newspapers to the glass and we turned off most of the lights in the house.

One of the jobs of the block captains was to quickly put out any kind of fire. For a practice run, a fire was built in the ditch beside the road in front of our house, and Daddy and several men used very little except their coats to smother and extinguish the fire. As Mama and Elaine and I watched the firefighters from our living room window, Mama gave us a complete explanation. She spoke softly, as though we might attract the enemy if she talked in a normal voice.

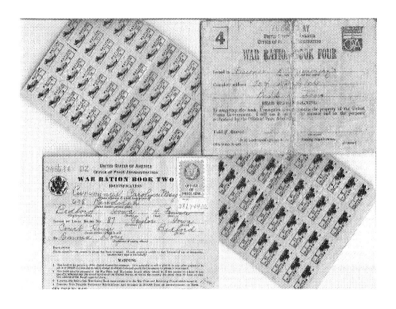

I remember feeling grown up and very responsible when I was allowed to lick the ration stamps and put them carefully into our ration books. We had books for gasoline and tires as well as sugar. We didn't go very far or very often in our black '39 Ford.

Daddy used a motorized bicycle to get to work, and Mom learned how to bake with less sugar. I don't recall hearing any conversation that sounded like someone was against the war effort. It seemed to me that everyone was united.

Our neighbor, Lester Johnson, looked so handsome in his uniform. My sister and I got to be photographed with him. His life was spared on December 7, 1941. He was on the USS Pennsylvania on that fateful day. He asked Daddy to drive him to town to catch the bus when he returned to active duty. As he told Daddy good-bye, he added, "Take care of my mother for me." Daddy could never retell that story with dry eyes. Mrs. Johnson saw all four of her sons again after the war was over. Sadly Mr. and Mrs. Tucker, who lived around the corner at Polk and Randolph Street, would never see their son David again. He was on the USS Arizona at Pearl Harbor in Honolulu, Hawaii. He died on December 7, 1941, 'the day that will go down in infamy.'

My first cousin, Bob O'Dell, served his country. He was in the Infantry. Mama told us that she thought of her oldest nephew every day, especially when we sat down to eat a meal. I'm sure that she prayed daily for his safety. I remember seeing a photograph of him in uniform at Aunt Josephine and Uncle Bruce's home. He was wounded by the time he was nineteen years old in the Battle of the Bulge in Germany.

A few of my kindergarten and first grade classmates disappeared for a few months as their families followed their Dads to military bases in other cities in the United States.

Our lives seemed sheltered and generally undisturbed by the war, but I think that was mostly due to my parents' careful screening when they spoke of war matters. One time Mama showed me a picture from the Sunday paper. The fear etched on the faces of the war victims stayed with me for a long time.

Then one day every bright red fire truck in Bedford turned on their sirens and drove around and around the streets of town. Firefighters, as well as servicemen that had returned from fighting, climbed on the trucks. There was yelling and celebrating everywhere. It was August, 1945, shortly before my seventh birthday. The trucks came down Randolph Street from both directions as Mama, Daddy, Elaine and I watched and waved from the front porch.

Now the favorite wartime songs that we sang around the piano could be enjoyed as musical memories instead of hopeful prayers for peace:

"When the Lights Come On Again All Over the World"

"There'll Be Bluebirds over the White Cliffs of Dover"

"Coming In On a Wing and a Prayer"

"Praise the Lord and Pass the Ammunition"

"Bell Bottom Trousers, Coat of Navy Blue"

Bedford was the home of several Purple Heart recipients. Although we wouldn't hear their stories for decades, we were proud of our heroes. The ration books, eventually, were not needed anymore. Factories turned out new home appliances, cars, and toys instead of ammunition. Women left the factory jobs and many returned to a different full time job at home.

We didn't need to practice blackouts any more. We took down the coverings from our windows.

A generation of *baby boomers* began to arrive.

Things began to return to normal.

But no one remained unchanged by that war.

Not even a little six year old girl in Iowa.

Monday Was Always "Warsh" Day

I wake up to the familiar sounds of the motor on the old Maytag wringer washing machine on the back porch. It must be Monday. Monday is Always Wash Day, or typically pronounced "warsh"day.

In the summer the back porch door would slam shut with frequency as Mom carried the bushel baskets of wet, clean clothes to the clothesline in the back yard. In the winter, the kitchen and bathroom and the enclosed back porch contained a rope clothesline crisscrossing overhead from hooks above the doorways, making the same cobweb pattern every Monday. These were the days before the electric clothes dryer. All of these sounds prepared me for what I'd encounter when I went downstairs. In the winter months, we became accustomed to eating our breakfast at the kitchen table, beneath the damp clothes hanging from Mom's creative indoor clothesline.

Long before I awoke, Mom sorted the week's dirty laundry into enormous piles on the floor of the back porch. The wash water had to be heated to a boiling temperature on the old black coal cook stove that stood in the northwest corner of the kitchen. The tall, black stovepipe towered above like an old black steam engine rumbling through the room. Mom had a large aluminum pot that held the water which she carried to the washing machine on the back porch.

When a shiny white electric range replaced the coal stove, Mom's work became a bit easier. With time and inspiration and an improved water heater, Mom rigged up a fitting to the faucet, attached a hose to it and snaked it out the kitchen door to the waiting washing machine on the back porch. It must have seemed like a luxury to her!

Into the filled washing machine tub of hot water would be placed a measured amount of Tide. Always Tide, in the bright orange and cobalt blue box. The first load was always Daddy's long-sleeved, white, cotton shirts, one for every day of the week. They agitated around in the machine after the gear shift was moved to high speed. If a load needed to be balanced, Mom used a long, smooth, wooden stick to relocate the clothes in the scalding hot water. Mom timed each load with her internal timer. She just knew. "It's time to wring these out into the rinse tub," she'd say to me. I thought the wringers were quite a fascinating invention but had been properly warned of their danger. When I grew tall enough to reach into the machine and start threading something through the wringers, Mom stood near by, guarding my small hands from the powerful rollers that pressed the moisture from the clothes.

As soon as the washing machine was emptied of load #1, the next pile of dirty clothes was placed carefully into the machine. Load #2 was another white load, such as a large white damask tablecloth or sheets and pillowcases. Sheets came in one color, and they were made of cotton, a fabric that would usually need ironing.

After the whites, the colorfast colors were washed. Sometimes another measure of Tide would be added to the wash water. Same water, just more detergent. The water would be cooled down to a warm temperature by this time.

As each load tumbled around in the washing machine, the previous load was swished through the cold water in the aluminum rinse tub. It stood on four legs but wasn't as tall as the washing machine, so I could reach into it easily. A liquid called *bluing* was added to the rinse water for the white loads. Then through another wondrous invention, the wringers could be released from their former position and pivoted at a ninety degree angle. Just the proper location to send the clothes through the wringers again, this time into the bushel basket on the floor.

Next, the clothes were hung on either the several lengths of wire line in the back yard or the rope line in the house. Each item was lapped over the line and secured in place with wooden clothespins. Mom always used the non-pinch kind. Mom made large clothespin bags from heavy ticking fabric or denim. Some of them were worn like an apron, tied around the waist. Some were just tied onto the clothesline.

Hanging the clothes outside in the warmer months was an opportunity to tune in to the sounds of nature. While birds sang in the tall trees, sounds from a cow or lamb or horse could be heard in the barnyard. Maybe a rooster would stretch his neck and crow as he marched about the chicken yard. There were always a few cats that wanted attention, rubbing against my legs and tangling themselves around my ankles. Tippy, our terrier, participated in back yard activity as long as someone would take the time to throw his ball for him.

There were understood rules about the proper order for hanging clothes. Similar items were pinned on the line next to each other. A shirt wasn't allowed next to underwear. It just wasn't done. All of the white shirts hung by the tail, upside down, next to each other. All of the socks were lined up, toe pinned to the line. I noticed this on other clotheslines around town. And the sheets and towels would be in front, hiding the underwear and less attractive wash from the neighbors driving by. Laundry on a line was a topic of conversation in town.

"My, Helen always has such a large laundry on Mondays."

Or "Doesn't Florence have a nice windy drying day for her clothes?"

In a small town it's hard to break out of the pattern that our mothers and grandmothers created. With the birth of the automatic clothes dryer, a whole topic of neighborhood conversation was wiped out.

I remember a few bad experiences when I got my small fingers and hands caught between the moving wringers of the old Maytag. Each time Mom flew to the rescue, disengaging the wringers with lightning speed. She deemed it a major tragedy, so I was always pleasantly surprised to find my hand was still in one piece. Mom overreacted sometimes.

The last loads of wash were Daddy's work clothes and the bib overalls. The gear shift on the side of the washing machine was moved to a slower speed. Finally, she'd toss in a few small throw rugs. By this time the water was a murky, black color. One could never accuse Mom of wasting water. She even made use of the wash water when the clothes were finished with it. In the summer heat, I'm sure Mom's flower beds and vegetable garden welcomed even the grungiest water.

Another feature of both washer and rinse tub was the draining hose. It was heavy work emptying the water through the hose into an aluminum bucket and carrying it outdoors.

The routine of wash day was monotonous...Monday after Monday. Strength and endurance were required. Amazingly, Mom could dovetail her homemaker duties with precision. By the time the last load of laundry was hanging on the line, she would have dinner prepared in the kitchen. The big meal of the day was eaten at noon at our house. Twelve o'clock sharp. The whistle at the Fire Station blew twice each day: 12 noon and 6 P.M.--like a call for everyone to gather at the watering hole. Pavlov's dog had nothing on the people of Bedford! Daddy's car would appear in the driveway like clockwork at 12:05. The routine of another Monday was acted out in homes all over our town.

Mom got an electric dryer sometime while Jimmie was still in diapers. What a washday helper for Mom!

If the unpredictable, ever-changing Iowa weather cooperated, the clothes could stay on the clothesline until they dried. But if it rained, fast tracks were made to rescue the clothes. Sometimes they just stayed on the line and got a second rinse! We just couldn't count on nature to behave every Monday, not in Iowa.

There were few things that escaped the heat of the iron on Tuesday. Another routine day. Another day of hard work. Before the ironing could be started, Mom had to sprinkle everything. Using an empty glass Royal Crown Cola bottle, Mom added a bottle top with holes in it. Filling the bottle with water, Mom sprinkled and dampened each item. Daddy's white shirts were starched and ironed to perfection. Elaine and I had yards of cotton material in our gathered skirts, and many more yards of crinoline or net in the petticoats (the uniform of the 1950s). However, by that time we were expected to do our share of the ironing.

Then in 1969, thirty-five years after Mom had been engaged in her Monday Maytag washing machine routine (the same machine all those years), she became the relieved and happy owner of an automatic Maytag washer. For the next twenty-eight years, it made my Mother's Monday routine a snap. The same Maytag automatic machine lasted almost thirty years. I doubt that there was an appliance, anywhere, anytime, that was appreciated as much. Mom deserved it.

Modern young homemakers don't know what they missed. They can see the old washing machines, wringers, and rinse tubs on display at the Taylor County Museum and thank their lucky stars that they were born too late!

There is a missing component to all of the modern day conveniences. Kids all over America are growing up without the childhood memories of the sounds, the routine, helping alongside Mom, the hard work, and the fresh smell of laundry drying outside on a clothesline.

It is hard to find anything that compares to the cool freshness of sheets and towels that have been clothesline-dried and whipped around by a strong Iowa breeze. That was the bonus at the end of another Monday, the day we called "warsh" day.

"Tiny" and the Dry Cleaning Truck

His name was Tiny, a tall, overweight, jovial gentleman who drove a white panel truck. The words ***Peerless Cleaners*** were printed on the side. Our town didn't have a dry cleaning establishment for a few years in the 1940s and 50s. So all of our dry cleaning was picked up by Tiny and hauled over to Clarinda, the next town west on Iowa's Highway 2. The clean clothes were returned the following week.

We didn't lock the doors of our homes in those days. Tiny knew the designated place inside everyone's front or back door. He was trusted by all of his customers.

Mom would hang a suit or coat in need of dry cleaning on the hall tree by the south entrance. Tiny would let himself in, calling out, "cleaners," whether anyone was home or not. He knew his established customers.

Tiny returned the following week with cleaned items under a paper covering on a wire hanger. If people were home, they honored his bill in person. But if not, he knew he could count on his customers sooner or later. Sometimes an established customer would leave cash on a table by the door. Or a signed, blank check might be left at the door, knowing that Tiny would fill in the proper amount, never a penny more.

I wish every kid in the world could have an opportunity to grow up in that kind of cocoon, where people trusted each other, where a person's word meant something, and where they learned the meaning of words like **honesty** and **trust** somewhere other than in the dictionary.

Dear Santa

Christmas was coming. Elaine and I didn't have really nice dolls. That's what we wanted. We wrote to Santa.

The war was over. It was December of 1945. Toys were in greater supply now that ammunition didn't top the list of manufactured goods in the country.

One day Elaine and I rode downtown with Mama and Daddy. They told us to stay in the back seat of their black 1939 Ford and wait for them. It was a safe request in those days. The only harm that could come to kids was what they might do to each other. Elaine and I would never do such a thing right there on Main Street in plain view of pedestrians and merchants.

We watched our parents come out of the Gamble Store with two boxes, each one a bit larger than a shoebox. They opened the trunk and placed them inside. When we returned home, the boxes stayed inside the trunk. Mama diverted our attention to other things. Elaine and I sized up the secretive situation and said nothing.

On Christmas morning we opened our gifts from Santa. Under the tree were two boxes, each one a bit larger than a shoebox. We opened them and found two beautiful dolls, exactly alike. We named them immediately. Elaine's doll was Susie and mine was named Betty. They were soft body dolls with the head, arms and legs sculpted from porcelain-like material. They did not have hair, just a suggestion of hair carved into their heads. They both had blue eyes that stayed open all the time. They didn't cry or wet or talk. We imagined all that.

Pink dresses and bonnets, the original outfits, were the only clothes they had for awhile. They were our first nice dolls, and we loved them well.

Five year old Elaine mentioned that the boxes seemed the same size as the ones we saw coming out of Gambles, but her ideas were quickly dashed by Mama, who still wanted us to be *believers.*

A few days after Christmas, Mom needed to go somewhere in the afternoon so she dropped us off at Aunt Nora's. Aunt Nora was our *Aunt* by name only. Mama had a big heart and shared her daughters with her friend who had no children.

Elaine had sized up the whole situation about the boxes and gifts from Santa and came up with her own theory, which she decided to share with Aunt Nora. In confidence, Elaine told her that she thought that parents were probably the real spirits of Santa Claus. "But," she cautioned Aunt Nora, "don't tell Carolyn. She doesn't know." Aunt Nora loved to tell that story.

My thoughts on Santa didn't change. I liked being a believer. I thought that was what kids were supposed to do. I didn't want to disappoint Mama and Daddy. Parents got a kick out of being Santa's gift givers. I think I hung on to the belief in Mr. and Mrs. Claus for, perhaps, another year.

I don't remember that Elaine and I had any discussions about Santa, and perhaps she didn't want to burst the bubble that I kept alive. Some things are better left unsaid.

Mama ordered doll wigs for Betty and Susie and gave them to us for Christmas the following year. Elaine chose a blonde wig for Susie. I wanted Betty to be a brunette.

Grandma O'Dell crocheted hats and booties and sweaters for our dolls. I still have those treasured gifts.

That same year Betty and Susie received new wardrobes from Santa. The packages were wrapped in familiar wrapping paper. A note from Mrs. Claus was pinned to several pieces of fabric cut in the shapes of tiny dresses and bonnets. The note was written in a handwriting that was identical to Mama's. It stated that since Mrs. Claus hadn't enough time to complete the clothes, perhaps our mother could finish sewing them. Dead give away! A turning point in my life!

After I sized up the situation, my little brain must have concluded that it was the right time to let Mama and Daddy in on my secret. Even though I felt guilty letting go of the tradition, I tried to let them down easily.

Decades later Mama rekindled the "spirit of Santa" and gave us a loving surprise. Betty and Susie had been put away for many years. Their clothes were faded, worn and wrinkled. The small wooden trunk of doll clothes had given most of the grandchildren hours of fun. The clothes had been worn by many cats, dogs, and dolls over the years. Betty and Susie's dresses were rescued from the trunk.

Mama washed the red satin doll dresses that she had made many years earlier. The dresses and bonnets were ironed with loving hands. They looked like new. The tiny buttons were replaced. New ribbons were sewn onto the bonnets.

In the early 1990s, Elaine and I were both home for Christmas at the same time. Quietly sneaking upstairs, Mama came down carrying Betty and Susie in their refurbished condition. Mama had a big heart. Her thoughtfulness was as priceless as Betty and Susie had become. With *lots of love* Mama had created a new and endearing memory. Forty-five years later, our restored antique dolls looked perfectly beautiful. How could I not believe in the spirit of Santa Claus?

Today Betty sits like a queen on a high shelf in my extra bedroom, the bedroom that has been christened Zoe's room.

Zoe was about to celebrate her first birthday when she saw my mother, her great-grandmother, for the first and last time.

She doesn't remember meeting my Mama, but she has only to look at Betty, and she knows my Mama's heart.

Summer Vacations

Ah! Just the sound of it brings memories of long, lazy days. But there was nothing lazy about our summer family vacation trips.

Daddy worked at the bank for fifty weeks each year. For his two weeks of vacation, he got into a car without air conditioning, two or three kids in the back seat, and drove hundreds of miles before returning home. That couldn't have been leisurely or lazy.

With an itinerary usually including a few days visiting relatives or friends, Mom carefully coordinated each day. She kept a log which included each day's mileage, where we "gassed up," and where we stayed each night. One of those logs was found when we went through the unoccupied house at *608 Randolph Street*. It was a very complete record of each state we visited, where we ate out (which was rare) and the time of arrivals and departures to various spots of interest. It was not a journal filled with thoughts, feelings, discoveries and ideas. Maybe Mom didn't have time to write a journal. She was in charge of food, kids, clothes in suitcases, records and lists, maps, and navigation. With only two weeks to cover our itinerary, we had to keep to a schedule which must have been exhausting for them.

I usually kept a diary, but finding some of those in the old house revealed that my diaries were much like Mom's logs. Facts only. We weren't taught to explore feelings and express opinions.

Water bags were hung over the hood ornaments of the cars in the 1940s, and frequent stops were made to add water to an overheated car. Of course, this was before air conditioning. Car windows were open during most of the trip. Bugs and flies were spattered over the front windshield, and sometimes they ended up inside the car. Driving in the mountains would often cause a car to vapor lock. If a car stalled on the highway, it usually didn't sit there too long before some kind Samaritan stopped to help. Flat tires were frequent. Delays were common. It took brave people with stern determination to make family car trips in the *olden* days.

Our family skimmed the surface of many wonderful places on our trips, never having enough time to be more than just a tourist in the fast lane. Mom and Dad would say to us, "Now you can say that you've been to the top of the Empire State Building," or "Now you can say that you've crossed the Continental Divide."

I guess one could conclude that we liked to hit the high spots!

Our lunches were usually eaten in our moving car. It saved time and money. We didn't have much of either. Before one of our family trips, Daddy constructed a wooden box with a hinged lid. This was about the size of a modern plastic storage box, but long before the time of plastic containers with tight lids. Daddy painted the box white, and we named it our food box. At the beginning of a summer trip, the box was packed with boxes of cereal, dry snacks, sandwich bread, peanut butter and cheeses, and probably some fresh fruit. Probably bananas--we ate lots of bananas! Knowing Mom's love for sweets, which she passed on to all her children, she packed cookies and sweet rolls inside.

When we were ready for lunch, Daddy would stop in a park or parking lot and unload the food box, climb back into the car, and continue driving to our next destination. Mom would make sandwiches on her lap and hand them back to Elaine and me in the back seat. After Jim came along, she'd pass him to the back seat for us to entertain while she performed her job as our cook. She'd pour a cup of coffee or cold drink for Daddy and hold it for him in between sips. This was before the days of handy cup holders and ledges on the dashboard. We loved to stop at grocery stores to get a *cold* drink and fresh supplies. What a treat to walk into a store that had a big sign on the front window that read: **Refrigeration Inside**! This was a forerunner to air conditioning.

In 1950 our family vacation trip included Yellowstone National Park, the Grand Teton Mountains, the Rocky Mountains, and Cheyenne, Wyoming, where Daddy's relatives put us up for the night and fed us elk. We stayed at Yellowstone Park for a night or two in a little log cabin next to all kinds of signs that read: **Please Do Not Feed the Bears.**

The next day while driving through the scenic park, we noticed lots of bears freely helping themselves to food arranged on picnic tables. There were no people in sight. What happened next was one of the times when Mom threw caution to the wind. Daddy stopped the car and pulled over to the side of the road. We wanted a closer look at the bears in action. Daddy didn't realize that Mom's passenger side window was down, all the way. A big brown bear ambled up to her window. He stood up on his back legs and placed his huge paw on the door. When Dad realized that Mom's window was down, he told her to roll it up *immediately*. But Mom playfully talked to the "nice ol' bear" taking her time to roll up the car window. Little Jimmie, two and a half years old, was standing in the front seat between Mom and Daddy, within easy reach of the nice ol'bear. That was our hair-raising excitement for that day.

Of course, no one goes to Yellowstone without watching the eruption of Old Faithful. We actually stayed around to watch Old Faithful geyser erupt twice. We walked around the smelly geysers and went into Old Faithful Lodge. A spectacular park, it is!

Little Jimmie stood up for most of that two week trip. Before the required car seat restraints for children, they had more freedom, along with more falls. Jimmie was an excellent traveler. He twirled around in the front seat and watched cars coming behind us as well as those that we met. He'd announce "nara nudder un" which meant "there's another one."

We heard our family mottos often during our car trips. Before jumping out of our parked car at a souvenir stand, Daddy would remind us that "Money doesn't grow on trees." When he was trying to round up his family to begin another day of traveling, he'd get us started with "Let's get this show on the road." We heard these two family mottos often.

Elaine and I entertained ourselves in the back seat with games, contests, singing, and watching the scenery. We looked forward to reading the popular progressive Burma Shave advertising signs spaced along the road. The signs whizzed by quickly. Elaine tried to read them all. Struggling to keep up with one of the rhyming ads and seeing the letters B and S on the last sign, she burst out with "Brown Shoes." She made a family memory at that moment.

One summer we crossed Kansas in the grueling August heat--over one hundred degrees in the shade. With the windows rolled down, Mom kept us supplied with wet washcloths to cool our skin. We went through several containers of water and fruit juices and drinks that day. We sat on beach towels over the hot car seats. It seems like it was anything but a vacation to me now. It seems more like an ordeal.

The guard at the Canadian border asked Daddy to open the trunk. His first question was, "What's in the box?"

"Food." Daddy's answer was succinct.

The guard lifted the lid and peered inside and found exactly that, food. With a nod of his head, he signaled our passage over the Canadian/U.S. border.

That summer we saw Wisconsin, Canada, Niagara Falls, and Mom's cousins in upstate New York. We had a personal guided tour of New York City from Mom's first cousin, Hugh Fitch, who lived in neighboring Leonia, New Jersey. We drove through New Jersey and into Pennsylvania where we took pictures of the crack in the Liberty bell in Philadelphia. We toured the White House, Capital Building and the Smithsonian Museum in Washington D.C. We walked to the top of the Lincoln Monument! With another cousin of Mom's, we had lunch at the Brookings Institute. Mt. Vernon was on our list of places to see and photograph. Crossing over the smoky Blue Ridge Mountains of Virginia and West Virginia, we headed west. We visited Lincoln country in Springfield, Illinois, and before driving home, made one more stop to visit relatives. Daddy's cousins, Uncles, and Aunts lived in Ottumwa and Bloomfield, Iowa. What a comprehensive experience for me to have before my eighth grade study of United States history! At that time, I never imagined that I would be a history teacher one day.

The service stations along the way actually gave service to their customers. I was fascinated with the variety of people who pumped gas. They asked for your personal choice of gas, regular or ethyl? Then they offered to check the oil and water levels. While the gas was pumping, we'd watch the different ways that a front windshield can be cleaned while enjoying the aroma of gasoline. We could usually talk Daddy into a bottle of cold soda from the huge, red, metal ice-filled chest inside the station. Just reaching into the icy-cold water was a treat on a hot summer day.

After a rest room stop, we'd be on the road again. Each town seemed different, but service stations brought a commonality to towns along the highways. They were welcome places where we could ask directions, chat about the weather, give a tired body a place to rest and stretch out the muscles that had taken on a permanent sitting position.

Mom kept track of things with her lists.

A list of all the states we had visited.

A list of all the family and friends we saw.

A list of the different license plates we'd seen.

A list of miles we traveled each day.

And a running list of gasoline and car expenses.

Every time a car was traveling faster than others, we concluded that that must be a California driver!

We traveled to more than half of the states in the United States during those family trips. I had a driver's permit for our summer trip up the North Shore drive of Lake Superior. I helped with the driving. Daddy was patient and quiet. Mom was a nervous back seat passenger! Elaine had developed a keen sense of humor by that time, so she kept Mom focused on lighter subjects.

We always took lots of pictures on every trip. Mom put them into photo albums in short order.

I think back to those family trips now from a parent's point of view, and I really appreciate the sacrifices that Mom and Dad made for those to happen. Mom would return home to a garden full of things that needed to be picked, preserved, canned, frozen, or pickled. Daddy would return to his daily routine at the bank during the day and tending to farm chores at home. They were never afraid of hard work. Our trips weren't as much a vacation for them as they were a change of scenery.

Jim continues with Mom's practice of trip structuring and scheduling. He has a goal for each day, knows what he wants to see along the way, and when he will arrive. Spontaneity is not part of his itinerary. He comes by that naturally!

At the end of a two week trip, we'd drive into Bedford and wonder if we had been missed. Grandma and Grandpa, next door, always took excellent care of things, including Tippy and the cats. They were our welcoming committee.

Mom would say, "Home, sweet, home," as we drove into our driveway. The house on the hill at *608 Randolph Street* always looked good to a family of tired travelers.

Baby Brother

I can remember exactly where I was standing in the kitchen when Mama asked my six year old sister and me IF we would like to have a baby sister or brother. It was a hot August day in 1947. I would soon turn nine years old. It was a canning day for Mama, and she had enlisted the help of her daughters. I was standing beside the kitchen sink, slipping off the fuzzy skins from the plump, blanched peaches in the sink.

This was a BIG day. We were happy to hear the news, though it was not quite believable. For years, Elaine and I had asked Santa for a baby brother or sister. We cut out baby pictures from the Sears & Roebuck and the Montgomery Ward catalogues and put them in envelopes and asked Mama to fill out order forms for a baby. We had become tired of asking. We were about to give up. So this was BIG news!

Then one morning in January 1948, our cousins Helen and Louise, woke us up instead of Mama. They helped us get ready for school. They were teenagers in high school, and they lived with us during the week and went to their home in the country on weekends. Bedford Public Schools did not yet have school buses to transport students from the country into town. Helen and Louise seemed like big sisters to Elaine and me. Their Aunt Helen's house was home to them for several months of the year. Grandma O'Dell lived with us, too. Emma May O'Dell was confined to her wheelchair and occupied the downstairs bedroom.

The date was January 14, 1948. Mama and Daddy had gone to the Clarinda hospital in the middle of the night. Wonder why so many babies decide to arrive at night or in the worst possible weather conditions?

When I arrived home from school that day, Daddy had not come back home yet. Aunt Neva was there, and I imagine she was quite anxious for some news. We all were.

Just before supper, Daddy arrived. We all met him at the back door. I still remember his wide smile and announcement: "It's a boy!" Cheers, yells, and clapping filled the air. There is just nothing like a wanted and long awaited baby.

New mothers had to stay in bed in the hospital for a week. I don't remember who stayed with us during that time. Probably Grandma Florence, Aunt Neva, Helen, and Louise.

Finally, the day arrived when Daddy drove Mama and baby James Carl Cummings home from the hospital. We all peered into the baby basket to admire a wrinkled newborn, just waking up and ready to eat.

Mama went to the sofa to lie down, something that we seldom saw her do. I don't remember lots of details of the first few days except that Mama couldn't eat chili and spicy foods because it would bother the baby. I wondered how he knew what Mama ate.

Jimmie was like a plaything, a doll or a toy. I think Elaine and I dressed him up in more doll clothes than we did the cats and kittens. We gave him rides in the baby buggy. In spite of Mama's protective care of Jimmie, we learned to entertain him and answer his cries.

Mama dealt with childbirth at the age of 41 remarkably well. I could sense how very special Jimmie was. It was apparent in the way that Mama and Daddy handled him and talked about him. Daddy's measure of pride with his son was something neither Elaine nor I could even compete.

There was no jealousy toward the newborn baby sibling. After all, Mama and Daddy waited a long, long time for Jimmie! Elaine and I did, too!

Chapter Six

Animals and Pets

Reigning Cats and Dogs

Canines

Elaine and I resorted to tears and it proved successful in the end. We even got three year old Jimmie into the act.

We had wanted a puppy for a very long time. Daddy was against having a dog. We *borrowed* a dog from Uncle Wilbur and Aunt Neva's farm for a trial run and named him Wiggles. He was a cute, medium-sized, long-haired dog who never stopped wiggling. One of his first activities was gathering up all of the boots and shoes from the doorsteps of every Randolph Street neighbor and bringing them to our back yard. Elaine and I had to find the owner of every stolen boot and shoe and return each one. Wiggles was a farm dog, and being attached to a leash on our clothesline just wasn't his style. Unfortunately, Wiggles freed himself from his leash and met his demise when the postal carrier ran over him on our street.

We kept up our relentless and tearful pursuit, going from Daddy to Mama and back to Daddy again. Daddy would say, "No." Mama would say, "Ask Daddy again," and Daddy would answer, "We'll see." We sensed they were beginning to weaken.

Then the neighbor family to the north bought a cute little terrier. Dickie Gamet brought Susie, his new puppy, over to our house. That cinched it.

When Dickie's dad told us where they bought Susie and that there was one little male puppy left from the litter, we really let out all the stops. We reasoned that with Jimmie's little playmate having a puppy, we couldn't imagine Daddy wanting his son to grow up without the companion of a little canine. We reminded Daddy that he had a terrific little dog named Buddy. We kept up the begging and pleading, probably a pathetic sight to watch. I think Mom probably worked on Daddy, too. It was, without a doubt, one of the happiest days of our childhood, when Daddy finally agreed that we could have a dog of our own.

The little dog had a five dollar price tag attached. Our next hurdle was to find the money. Elaine's bank and mine were nearly empty, but we each contributed one dollar toward the cause. Jimmie's bank was full of money. Elaine reasoned that since Jimmie was three years old, his portion should be three dollars. We could talk him into anything. With our money collected, all five of us drove to a farm near Gravity, Iowa, where the little dog was waiting for his new family. He was bigger than his sister Susie. Mostly white in color, he had a brown tipped left ear and brown color around his left eye. Tippy was finally ours, and we were absolutely thrilled! It didn't matter that Elaine and I were each only one-fifth owners!

Our little dog was probably the most pampered dog in town. He was rocked to sleep, given rides in the doll buggy, held like a baby, dressed in Jimmie's baby clothes, and his photographs and measurements were kept in his Baby Book, one of the things found in the house. Mom had carefully saved it all those years.

Our parents insisted that Tippy be an outdoor dog. The chicken house had been converted into a playhouse for us kids by that time, so we moved some furniture there for Tippy. He had his own house. That's where he slept. Lucky little dog. We treated Tippy like royalty.

He easily learned tricks. He could retrieve a ball and climb a ladder. He followed along when we rode our bicycles and ran beside the horses when we went horseback riding. Tippy was loved. I think even Mom and Daddy came to love him too.

Eventually, Tippy wore his teeth down to the gums because he loved to retrieve. The most available objects for him to retrieve were gravel rocks from our driveway and pine cones from the front yard.  He would drop a rock or pine cone at the feet of anyone, family or visitor, hoping they would become engaged in a game of toss and retrieve. Cousin Ben Rankin remembered how Tippy placed a pine cone behind a person's fanny when sitting outside in a lawn chair. He continued to nudge and push until the human was nearly pushed from the chair. Tippy knew how to get attention. The hard toys ground away at his teeth, but he continued to play his favorite game.

Although Tippy was always an outdoor dog, he *wintered* on the back porch the last year of his life. Mom and Dad had compassion for him as he grew older.

I lived in California when Mama wrote to tell me that Tippy was gone. He had had a good life, belonged to a loving family, and lived to be about 12 years old. Tears were shed that day, and I missed him the next time I went back to visit the folks at *608 Randolph Street*.

Tippy was the first of other special dogs that have owned me. I can't imagine being without a furry companion. They continue to teach me valuable lessons of love, loyalty, peace, patience, and faithfulness. By example, they make good teachers!

Lula Belle and other Felines

Lula Belle was our best cat. She was tame, friendly, patient with children, and gave us a new litter of baby kittens every spring. She was an ordinary spotted barn cat, but she was never ordinary to us. She allowed us to play with her babies from the first day. She was a survivor and lived a longer life than most outdoor cats.

Some of the felines were trusting and had gentle dispositions. They let us dress them in bonnets and doll clothes. Others liked to ride in the doll buggy or in a wagon.

At one time we counted thirteen felines that came running from the barn and jumping out of trees when they heard the familiar call, "Here, kitty, kitty, kitty."

Many of them weren't tame and hung out in the barn most of the time. It is beneficial to have a few good "mousers" living in a barn. Occasionally we would discover a hidden litter of kittens among the bales of hay or in a box somewhere. We loved surprises like that.

One day Elaine and I were playing in our car, pretending we were going on a trip. We had imaginations that took us anywhere, any time. I was in the driver's seat, and Elaine was sitting in the passenger seat. An old white barn cat decided to jump into the back seat of the '39 Ford and give birth to a litter of kittens. We heard a growling noise in the back seat, and with eyes wide open, we watched our first birth experience. We quickly reported the incident to Mom who lifted the tiny creatures and their mother cat from the car. She acted somewhat embarrassed and disgusted that the white cat had chosen a blanket on the back seat of our car to give birth.

Our cats had to survive the winters, predators, and disease. Most of them didn't live long lives, which was normal for outdoor cats on a farm. They weren't taken to the veterinarian every year for shots and an annual exam. From these barn cats I learned to admire animals, and I have had at least one pet most of my life.

Recent Reigning Royalty

My children, Cathy and Steve, and I are still rescuing cats and dogs. Our pets are treated like royalty. All of my cats curl up in a chair in the atrium where they sleep all day in the sunshine enjoying the good life. I rescued them from neglect and abandonment; I think they remember that. They remind me daily of what is really important: things like loyalty, showing appreciation and affection, being patient and calm.

Two dogs, Orpha and Scruffy, lived with Cathy, Steve, and me for thirteen and sixteen years, respectively. Like members of our family, they had Christmas stockings and presents under the tree, and in some uncanny way they knew which ones were theirs. They weren't large dogs, but they knew how to protect us against intruders, meter readers, and mail carriers. They learned and performed tricks, always trying to please us. They enjoyed parties given in their honor at birthday time. They acted almost human at times. Their intelligence and unending devotion amazed us. They offered companionship, and they left us with many fine stories, warm memories, and hundreds of photographs.

My pets trust me with everything, even with the most difficult decision, knowing when it is time to say "Good bye." Staying with them until the end has seemed like such a small thing, albeit difficult, to do for these wonderful creatures that have given so much unconditional love and loyalty and left lasting (paw) prints on my heart.

God made the animals first. Maybe that's because animals have a lot to teach us humans.

Jimmie's Pet Calf

Jimmie had a pet calf that followed him around in the barnyard. He would sit down in the pasture, and the calf would come to him and lay his head in Jimmie's lap. He even put a saddle on the calf and rode him around the barnyard. The special little calf's name was Buttercup. They had a bonded relationship like a special one I read about once in a book called *Every Dog Needs a Boy*.

When Buttercup became sick, Dr. Don Anderson, DVM, tried to heal him, but the little calf didn't survive. It was through this experience that Jimmie made a decision to become a veterinarian.

As a tender little kid about eight years old, Jimmie wasn't ready to say good-bye to his pet. He decided to have a funeral for his calf. Planned all by himself, he asked Mom and Daddy and his two big sisters to place the lawn chairs in the back yard facing west. I remember that there was an outstanding sunset that evening. Our chairs were placed around the huge tractor tire sandbox where Jimmie had placed a handmade wooden cross. The two plum trees on each side of the sandbox gave a finished setting for the service.

On this solemn occasion, Jimmie recited the Twenty-third Psalm, and I don't remember the rest. It tore at my heart, and it must have touched Daddy and Mom's, also. This was the first time I saw Daddy's eyes fill with tears and run down his cheeks. Mom was wiping her eyes with her apron. The healing process began with Buttercup's funeral.

Jimmie became Dr. James Cummings, DVM. His practice began with Dr. Don Anderson, who had begun his practice with his father, Dr. T. E. Anderson. Many years later, this story was part of a eulogy that Jim read at the funeral of Dr. Don Anderson, his mentor, his partner, and his long time friend.

The seventh chapter of Ecclesiastes, verse 11 in the New International Version of the Bible reads, "Sorrow is better than laughter, for sadness has a refining influence on us." A single event can shape a life as that one influenced Jim's.

Although this story happened a long time ago, I'm sure Jim thinks of it often. And I bet he will pass this story on to his grandkids when they ask, "Papa, why did you become a veterinarian?"

On Top of Ol' Smokey and Other Equines

My little sister Elaine and I were not experienced at riding horses. Not like Mom. When she was a kid, she rode standing up. Then she and her brother learned to stand on the backs of two horses, one foot on one horse and the other foot on another. Roman style, it's called. She and her brother were daring. Elaine and I were not. But we liked to think we could hold our own on the back of a horse.

There were several horses on our acreage. Daddy's first two favorites were Ginger and White Sox.

I remember riding White Sox once. When Daddy thought I was strong enough to control him, he helped me into the saddle. I headed west, out into the pasture, with a goal to actually keep White Sox headed west until I reached the fence line and the end of our property. He must have been as suspicious of me as I was of him. Daddy always said that White Sox was a one-man horse, and he knew that I wasn't his *one man*. He was the tallest horse I'd ever mounted. It would be a long way down if I fell off of his back. I pretended to be in control of my horse as we picked up speed going across the small creek and up the other side of the pasture. White Sox looked like Black Beauty, with four white feet and a white star in the middle of his forehead.

Upon reaching the west fence line, I had a moment to feel proud of my accomplishment. But that lasted only for a moment. White Sox had his own ideas about who would be in control of the return trip back to the barn. As soon as we turned to face east and he could see the barn in the distance, he decided to take off. I hung onto the saddle horn and his mane, secured my feet into the stirrups, hunkered down close to his neck, and watched the fence posts speed past. As I bounced up and down in the saddle, I didn't pull back on the reins. I didn't say "Whoa, Horsey," or "Stop." I just hung on. The return trip to the barn seemed ever so quick. Daddy watched the whole episode. He was probably as relieved as I was that I had somehow managed to stay on the back of his horse. He complimented me on my first ride on White Sox, but I never asked to ride him again.

Elaine and I wanted a pony. Uncle Herman had several ponies on his farm. He loaned us an older horse with a slightly swayed back and a stubborn disposition. His name was Smokey. We had the use of him for several months. Putting a bridal on Smokey was a challenge because he had sensitive ears. We'd put the saddle blanket over his back and hoist the army saddle up and over, cinching it around his wide girth, and then we'd be ready to mount.

Carolyn, Elaine, and Jimmie on top of Smokey

There was a mulberry tree at the west edge of our pasture. On warm summer days when we could coax Smokey to go that far, we'd give ourselves a treat. We could reach the branches of the mulberry tree if we stayed on top of old Smokey. What could be better on a lazy summer day than being outside smelling the tall pasture grass, hearing an occasional groan that only a leather saddle can make, and eating mulberries right off the tree?

Some days we'd set out on Smokey and go onto the country roads behind our house. We felt safe on Smokey because he had one speed...slow! Uncle Herman had cautioned us about Smokey's one fear. He was afraid of the big yellow road graders that frequently leveled off the secondary dirt and gravel roads of Taylor County, Iowa.

One day, with Elaine riding behind me on the back of old Smokey, we ventured out west over the rolling Iowa hills and curving country roads. On our way back home, we saw Smokey's number one enemy popping up over the hill behind us. Not knowing how fast the road grader was approaching, I began to panic. Poking my heels into Smokey's sides and yelling, "Giddyup, Horsey," I tried to get him to trot or gallop, or something, anything faster. The best Smokey could do was manage a lazy trot, which kept Elaine bouncing from side to side, fearing a fall with each bounce. "Giddyup, Smokey. Our lives depend on it!" I yelled. I don't know how my little sister stayed on during that ride. Neither does she. Fortunately, we made it back home long before the yellow road grader rolled past our house.

We laugh about it now, and I can still remember how Uncle Herman laughed his long rolling laugh when Elaine told him what I had said.

Daddy, Uncle Herman, and my cousin, Keith, were charter members of the Bedford Saddle Club, which grew in numbers every year. They rode in parades in Bedford and other small towns in southwest Iowa. Uncle Herman was in the Taylor County Sheriff's posse.

Little brother Jim always had a pony to ride when he was growing up. Recently Jim recalled a rescue race that he and our cousin, Keith, entered at the fairgrounds one summer. The year was about 1970. The horse was old Ruthie, one of Keith's fastest mares. The goal of the rescue race was for the horse with rider number one to run through obstacles to the end where rider number two waits to mount, before rounding the bend and returning to the starting line. Being a timed event, speed was the name of the game.

Attempting to leap onto the back of the horse behind rider number one is the object of rider number two. Jim was rider number two. For a faster time, it is better to keep the horse in motion rounding the bend, letting the centrifugal force of the moving horse help the rider mount. Jim was young and agile, able to make this running leap. The final part of the race was when the riders attempted to ride double back to the starting line. Jim and Keith won the rescue race that day on the back of old Ruthie. Jim and Keith have the ability (perhaps it's inherited) to enhance this story each time it is told.

Uncle Herman built a *chariot* using some car wheels, a short axle, and the bottom half of a fifty-five gallon wooden barrel. I've already mentioned that Uncle Herman was a colorful character. Did he ever know how to have fun! Uncle Herman drove this contraption in parades around the county and entered it in the *chariot* races at the fairgrounds. It took two horses to pull the *chariot*, and he used old Ruthie and Daddy's horse, White Sox. With this winning team, Uncle Herman was declared the winner of the *chariot* races! Sometimes certain horses become a legend in their own lifetime. Word got out that day that two of the fastest horses in Taylor County had performed right there at the fairground race track in front of a homemade *chariot*.

Horses were a great source of entertainment for the family and friends that were neighbors west of Bedford. They made their own fun and loved to challenge each other in various pursuits, horse races being one of them. Horse stories were shared and enjoyed, and they just might have been embellished now and then. There were some real characters in this group of storytellers! When I was a child, this group of neighbors got together annually to celebrate the Fourth of July with fireworks in the evening and several freezers of homemade ice cream, plus a huge spread of desserts. They called themselves "the gang." That ought to tell you something!

Doyle Cooper, known as Dooley, talked Uncle Herman into riding in a half-mile race at the fairgrounds one summer. The announcer called for the horses and their riders to prepare for the next race. Dooley was riding his horse, Sonny. Dad's horse, White Sox, was tied to a stake near the judges' stand where Dad was working as a scorekeeper. Uncle Herman thought White Sox would be a winner, so with Dad's permission, White Sox entered the race. And what a race it was! Sonny and White Sox were in the lead rounding the final curve. Dooley was holding Sonny back, wanting to let Uncle Herman have a chance to claim the victory, but White Sox had other ideas. Just before he reached the judges stand, he suddenly jumped the hub rail and went back to his stake! The race was over for him. Uncle Herman just threw back his head and laughed and laughed. Dooley and Sonny were declared the winners of the half mile race. Watching from the judges' stand, Daddy was amused at the speed, strength, and stubbornness of his horse, pretty much in that order!

Pedro was a little black horse that Elaine rode on a Saddle Club trail ride. She was using an army saddle for that ride, a hard leather saddle with a hole down the center of the seat. Nearing the end of the ride, her backside was giving her much pain, so she decided to get off the horse and walk along beside Pedro to the trail's end. So much for that trail ride!

Jim had a little spotted pony named Lucky when he was in sixth grade. He remembers riding Lucky around town after school. Being able to saddle and bridal the horse by himself gave him a sense of grown-up accomplishment.

Then Daddy sold White Sox and bought Tuffy, a buckskin horse with a gentle disposition. This little horse was specifically for the grandchildren who were coming along by this time.

Jeckity and Buster were the last two ponies that Dad bought. Both small in size, they could be harnessed together to pull a small cart. Friends, neighbor kids, and grandchildren loved to ride in the cart.

There are still horses at 704 Randolph Street today. My brother, Dr. Jim, DVM, raises Standardbred horses and has brought the art of harness racing back to our hometown. Once a year, folks come from near and far to see the harness races at the Taylor County Fairgrounds.

Jim's latest winner is a three year old filly named Cyclone May. The name Cyclone represents the name of Jim's Alma Mater, Iowa State University, and May gives honor to our mother, one of Southwest Iowa's most accomplished horsewomen of her time. Born on May 16th, the little filly came into this world on the anniversary of Mom's death. Winning thirteen of her first sixteen races in the 2006 and 2007 seasons has made her a favorite in the state of Iowa. She's won blankets, trophies, and money. She starts from behind and makes her move along the back stretch. Jim thinks she knows exactly where the finish line is! We've been entertained and surprised by Cyclone May. As Daddy always said, "You just never know about a horse race. Anything can happen."

A late notation (2008) about the horses in Jim's pasture at 704 Randolph Street:

Cycle May is assuming the role of surrogate mother to the newest colt, Cyclone Ben. The mother of Ben and May died about a month after Ben was born. Cyclone May might have run her last race. She will foal in the spring of 2009. We're hoping for more Cyclones and more exciting races in the future. "You just never know about a horse race. Anything can happen."

Bounce and Lucy

Sometimes when a mother sheep dies or for some reason disowns one of her baby lambs, the orphaned animal needs tender loving care and a bottle every four hours. Farmers and their wives get up in the middle of the night to bottle feed a lamb or other struggling baby animal.

When word got out around town that Carl Cummings and his son Jim would take on the job of rescuing and raising an orphaned animal, several calls came in.

The first little orphaned lamb was given the name of Bounce. Jim named her as he watched her move around the barnyard on four springy legs. Her home was the old chicken house which had been moved into the barnyard area. We gave her the bottle and watched the milk run from the corners of her mouth as she tipped her head back and devoured the warm liquid. Those noises made by a baby human or animal let you know that they are really enjoying the contents of the bottle. I loved to run my fingers over her kinky, wooly coat, but most of all I loved to hear her vibrating voice let out a small "baaaaa."

A short time after we got Bounce, another call came about an orphaned lamb. Grandpa Clyde and Mama drove to a farm to pick up the lamb. Her tiny body was lying on the cold ground, and Grandpa started to walk away thinking she was dead. Then Mama saw the tiny body quiver, perhaps a last desperate cry for help. Mama believed the lamb could be saved. The tiny animal was wrapped in a blanket, carried to the car, and given a place of highest priority in the house. She was placed in a box on the heat register in the kitchen. Then Mama did something that we had never seen her do before. She went to the pantry and came out with a bottle of brandy, used for medicinal purposes only! Warming a small amount of the beverage, Mama got some down the lamb's throat. Mom didn't have much hope that the lamb could survive, but within a day's time, the little lamb was able to stand up in her box. Regular bottle feedings and warm surroundings and, of course, the dose of brandy seemed to jump start the tiny creature. We named her Lucy. She enjoyed the shelter of the back porch for a few weeks, a privilege few animals ever experienced. I believe that Mama and Lucy had a unique bond during those weeks.

Jim remembers that when the back porch began to take on the familiar odors of a barnyard, Mom declared Lucy well enough to venture into the outside world.

When Lucy joined Bounce in the barnyard, we became aware that Lucy was partially blind. Lucy could run around the barnyard like a sighted animal as long as one side of her face was touching the side of Bounce. The two of them ran in circles around the barnyard, always keeping their bodies close together like a team of horses in a harness.

When market day came, and it always did for farm animals, Elaine, Jim, and I dealt with the news with mixed emotions. Living in denial when the baby animal was little and helpless allowed us to enjoy their cuteness. Knowing the day would come when an animal was placed in a truck and taken away prevented us from bonding too closely.

Jim recently shared with me the financial arrangements that were made after the sale of Bounce and Lucy. I didn't remember any of that. Jim received the money from the sale of one of the lambs. He believes that he was the recipient of the money because he originated the idea of rescuing orphaned animals. What Daddy did with the profit from the other lamb, Jim doesn't remember.

Somewhere in this conclusion I can deduct two things:

First, Jim had experience with animal welfare at an early age. This prepared him for a long career of helping animals; and second, you never know when an idea might have a monetary reward. It couldn't have happened to a better guy, who just happens to be my "liddle brudder," and just possibly the favorite child!

When we were cleaning out the house at *608 Randolph Street* that summer of 2003, Jim found the old bottle of brandy still on the back of a pantry shelf, nearly fifty years after Lucy had been revived by its *healing* contents!

Somehow, that doesn't surprise me at all!

Chapter Seven

Favorite Lines and Stories

Every family has treasured memories. Here are a few of our family's favorite stories, as I remember them.

Cracks in the Belfry

Being available and willing to serve on many church projects, Daddy was put in charge of finding the finances to repair the belfry of the Methodist Church. He first learned of this appointment just before the 11:00 A.M. Sunday service. I'm sure Daddy must have prayed for Divine help on this.

Typical of Iowa's ever-changing weather conditions, a storm came up out of the southwest during the service. The sky turned a ghastly shade of green, followed by a downpour and winds that were fierce enough to cause damage to structures throughout the town, and the belfry of the Methodist Church sustained considerable damage.

The insurance company covered the total cost of the belfry repair!

July Third Wedding

Performing wedding ceremonies was one of Daddy's pastoral responsibilities. I think he enjoyed these more than any other duty.

Bill and Jane wanted Daddy to perform their wedding at a little white country church named Rose Hill. It sat on a hill north of Clarinda and looked like a Norman Rockwell painting.

On the day of the rehearsal, the weather was typical of Iowa's unrelenting heat. In July it is too hot, extremely humid, and just plain miserable, especially in a little church with no air-conditioning. With a wink and a grin, Daddy promised that he would pray for a breeze on the day of the wedding.

I drove Mom to the picture-perfect little church on the big day. As we got out of the car, a strong wind blew our dresses up to our necks, and it slammed the car doors shut while we were still trying to get out. I held on to Mom, fearing she might become airborne. The hot wind, blowing across the Iowa fields of corn, gained momentum and reached top speed at the crest of the hill.

The father of the bride, affectionately called "Gif" met us outside the front door. Gif retold the promise that Dad had made the day before. With a wink and a grin, he said, "Your Dad said he'd pray for a breeze, but I had _no_ idea!"

Cast Your Bread

Our Grandma Florence seldom went shopping for herself. She didn't seem to need much.

Once when the Baptist Church had a rummage sale, she donated three dresses from her closet.

Within a few days a package arrived for Grandma in the mail. It came from Omaha and was a gift from Blanche. Upon opening the package, it contained three new dresses.

Grandma loved to tell this story and always ended with, "Cast your bread upon the water, and it will come back, buttered on both sides."

(Thanks, Elaine, for remembering this treasured story about Grandma.)

Daddy Collected Things

Daddy was a collector. He had a drawer full of pocket knives. Handles of stone or mother of pearl or shell, they were all sizes and manner of blades. From his first pocketknife, given to him by his father when he was thirteen, to his last one found in an antique shop, he could remember where each one originated. Some were gifts, many were inherited from old friends, and some were just for collecting.

Mom dreaded Daddy's trips to estate sales. He would come home with boxes or paper bags full of things. He liked old books, paper bags of dusty, aging books. They began to fill the bookcases upstairs. There were complete sets of resource books, complete works by certain authors, books by inspirational authors, and occasionally, something that he actually read.

Besides the old books, Dad had quite a library. Most of his books were given to him. He read most of them. Among the cherished old textbooks were his own junior high textbooks: *General Hygiene*, copyright in 1913; *Mace's School History of the United States,* 1904; *Robinson's Complete Arithmetic*, 1901*; The Bender Primer*, published in 1907, the year in which Dad was born. They sit on one of my bookshelves now.

Daddy liked tools. At one time, Jim counted seven hammers in Dad's toolbox. He liked gadgets, some for fixing things and some for kitchen use and some just for collecting.

Daddy liked canes, and he collected those too. In later years, he used one to steady his walk. With more time on his hands than ever, Daddy needed a craft. He never liked to throw away something that might be useful someday. So, instead of throwing away old wooden broomsticks, they were turned into walking canes. Daddy whittled and sanded the sticks for hours, then crafted a handle for the top of the stick. He gave away most of the seventy canes he made. Frank Jones carried one on his daily journey from one end of

Main Street to the other. You might say that Frank was Daddy's sales rep. They were trusted, respected, life-long friends. When Frank showed the cane to the folks on Main Street, he'd let them know that "Carl Cummings can make one for you, too." Frank brought orders to Daddy, and Daddy produced more canes.

Daddy collected Studebakers. He and Boyd Novinger shared a common interest in the cars and enjoyed helping each other buy and sell these vehicles. Many of them were cleaned and polished before Dad drove them in the Fourth of July Parade in town. At one time my Dad had eight vehicles, all running well, with insurance and registrations in force. Most of them were Studebakers, models from 1950s and 60s. Mom always worried that if Daddy would go first, she would never be able to unload all those old cars. But that wasn't the case in the end. Mom never had to worry about that. Daddy sold most of them himself, and Jim found buyers for the last ones on the internet.

Daddy saved newspapers announcing great moments and events in history. This stack of papers was found in an upstairs closet, a surprise to all. They ended up at the Taylor County Museum.

Every ballpoint pen that advertised a business in Bedford, past and present, had been kept in a drawer. Pens that no longer worked told about another era, of stores no longer open, or the anniversary of a long time family business.

Old postcards from all over the world told their stories about friends and family and their travels. Daddy had saved them all. His collection of matchbooks filled another drawer.

The Depression played a part in my parents' saving habits. Perhaps these keepers explain, in part, his clear memory for details.

I can still hear Daddy say, "I'd better save that. It might be just exactly what I'll need some day."

Feeling Your Age?

Carla went to see her Grandpa Carl after he had triple by pass heart surgery. At the age of ninety, it was a somewhat risky procedure. He was happy to report that he felt great.

"Why, Carla, I feel almost like I'm seventy," he said with a smile!

The Birthday Present

When we were quite young, Elaine and I went shopping all by ourselves to find a birthday present for Daddy. The S and G Store (the local five and dime) was always a popular and safe place for little kids to shop. We selected a hairbrush for him, a surprising gift since Daddy had precious little hair on top. I wonder what we were thinking.

Before we wrapped it, we had to try out the brush. We liked the way it felt moving over our long blonde locks.

We had kept our gift selection a secret from Mom too. Feeling quite proud of ourselves, we waited with great anticipation while Daddy opened his gift. He seemed to be surprised when he saw the brush, but had a quick expression of appreciation. "Oh my, a hair brush! Now that's something I can really use, and I appreciate the hair in it, too!" All said without a smile, of course. Mom laughed enough for both of them. She liked his dry wit. They were good sports.

Howdy Neighbor

My children would be the first ones to notice it. They didn't grow up in Iowa so it was unfamiliar to them. They noticed the special wave that drivers of pick up trucks use, whether meeting on the highways, country roads, or at intersections in town.

Keeping both hands visible near the top of the steering wheel, the straight index finger of one hand is lifted two or three inches off the wheel. That is all; only one finger moves. Sometimes the driver gives a slight nod of the head as the finger is lifted.

Most of the farmers around a small town are familiar with the kind of pick up or car other farmers and residents drive. But recently I've noticed that the special wave is not reserved for familiar faces and vehicles. Being an out-of-towner in an airport rental car, no one has any idea who I am; even so, I've received the farmers' friendly finger wave. It appears that the sociable gesture knows no discrimination. It reinforces my belief that the Midwest is full of friendly people.

The kids didn't need a map. Near the end of our trips to Iowa, one of them would say, "Hey, Mom, there's the finger wave. We must be getting close to Grandma and Grandpa's house."

Uncle Herman

Mom's brother, my Uncle Herman, had a way of summing up a situation.

On one occasion when eating at a restaurant, he ordered his steak well done--very, very well done. Uncle Herman's steak came back to his table with a small amount of pink color oozing from the steak. In sending it back to the kitchen for more cooking, he summed up the condition of the steak like this, "I've seen cows hurt worse than that get better."

More Uncle Herman

Being brave travelers, Uncle Herman and Aunt Doris made several trips by car to Southern California to see their daughter Cheryl. They wasted no words in sharing their dislike of California freeways. Uncle Herman had this to say about the freeways, "That's just a race track out there. I like to see a finish."

The few times that I heard my Dad really burst out laughing was because of something that Uncle Herman said. Theirs was a close relationship, and they shared a mutual respect throughout their lives. When Daddy married Mom, he also acquired the brother that he never had. Daddy outlived most of his friends and family, but I think Daddy missed Uncle Herman more than anyone after his untimely passing at the age of only seventy-seven.

Loyal Friends

Daddy had many long-time, loyal friends who visited him weekly after Mom was gone. Harold Shepherd, Bob Stacy, and Frank Jones are just three of them. It seems appropriate to include a short story about each of them.

The Song

One Sunday morning Harold Shepherd was in charge of the opening exercises at the Methodist Church. He was leading the singing of the old hymn, "Rescue the Perishing." The cadence was very slow, fiercely out of character for the

Methodist Church where the hymns usually galloped along at a pretty fast clip. Bob Stacy strolled into the office where Daddy was working and shared his thoughts: "I don't believe Harold is going to get the perishing rescued this morning." Daddy and Bob appreciated each other's subtle wit and dry humor!

(Thanks to Jim, for sharing that story with me.

He, also, shared the following story of a fishing trip with the Shepherd family)

The Fish

In the early 1960s Dad and Jim did a lot of fishing together. Harold and Denny Shepherd joined them frequently for a father-son activity. On one particular occasion Mom and Velma went along for the fun of it. There was a farm pond west of town owned by Wilbur Sleep, and that's where this story happened.

No one had caught anything when suddenly Mom hooked a nice three or four pound bass. She landed him, but before she could get her hands on the fish, he spit out the hook and began flopping around on the bank. Dad rushed to help get the fish on the stringer. Mom began yelling, "Oh, Carl. Get 'em. Get 'em." Dad got down on his hands and knees trying to reclaim the fish by tackling it like a football. About the time he reached the evasive fish, it would flop again, each time getting closer to the water's edge. Mom continued her chant, "Get 'em, Carl. Get 'em." When the fish flopped back into the water, Dad crawled after it. Dad was up to his elbows in water, with the fish one flop ahead of him. Dad reached, the fish flopped. This continued until Dad was up to his neck in deep water. Mom sounded disappointed, "Oh, Carl. Oh, my." Dad had to abandon his gallant attempts to catch the fish. He swam a few strokes back to shallow water and waded out of the pond.

Harold, Velma, Denny, and Jim watched this performance from the other side of the pond. Dad sauntered back to their side where his audience was trying to keep from laughing. Harold spoke first, "Well, Cummins, I see you've had your hydrotherapy for the day."

The Teacher

Frank Jones had a way with words. His funeral program contains these words: He practiced his hobby of farming in order to afford to carry on his avocation of talking and taking trips.

Besides being Daddy's "sale representative" for his hand made canes, he liked to tell this story over and over:

My mother was his teacher at the one room school house called the Jones School. My mother, Miss O'Dell, was only five years older than Frank. He said she was his favorite teacher because she would go out and play with everyone at recess time. When she threw a ball, she had a mean overhand toss.

Sixty-some years later Frank still loved to tell this story about his favorite teacher, Miss O'Dell.

More Favorite Lines and Stories

Dad's Favorite Old Cardigan

After Daddy retired from the bank, he climbed into more casual attire. He acquired a real Perry Como look, wearing comfy cardigans for the first time in his life. He had a favorite old blue cardigan. Each time I'd visit, Daddy would start with, "Honey, I've been saving this for you to do," as he brought out the old blue cardigan. "The buttons are loose again and the buttonholes are too big. Think you can fix it?"

I'd reinforce the buttonholes and attach the buttons with buttonhole twist, making a thread shank behind each button. Sometimes the seams needed re-stitching. Dad's old cardigan was literally holding on by a thread! But, in spite of numerous gifts of cardigans, Daddy kept his favorite blue one. No other cardigan was as endearing to Daddy as that one. As he got thinner, it became a close, comfortable layer against his body, and it must have felt like the embrace of an old, old friend.

Dad's Favorite Plate

Jim, Elaine, and I decided that Mom and Daddy needed some new everyday china. They were using mismatched plates, leftovers from several sets of china and estate sales. So for an anniversary gift we bought a set of Corelle, service for eight; matching cups, bowls, salad and dinner plates, serving dishes, the whole thing. Really nice.

As Mom and Dad unwrapped the gift, they showed polite appreciation but said they didn't really think they needed more dishes.

Elaine and I boxed up the old mismatched dishes, including one pink Melmac dinner plate that Daddy found somewhere at an estate sale. We placed the box in the store room upstairs. This act was very revealing of the fact that my sister and brother and I must have inherited some of those saver and keeper genes!

We washed the new china, stacked some in the china cabinet above the sink and set the table with the others. It looked good. A matched set!

Daddy had one question when he saw the table. "Now where did you put the old ones, just so I'll know? I kind of liked that old pink plate."

A few weeks later I noticed the pink plate was back in the china cabinet above the sink!

Mom was a Risk-Taker

Mom had incredible agility and physical strength. Her feats of courage and endurance surprised us all the time. She could build a pair of stilts and maneuver them around the back yard like a pro. Even wearing her usual oxford heels, she'd climb on the things and make it look easy.

When Mom and her little brother Herman were kids, they had twin ponies to ride. They learned to ride them Roman-style, standing on the backs of the ponies. What a risk-taker!

I saw Mom scale a fence with the agility of an Olympic gymnast. She was in her early eighties.

Daddy and Wayne Harbour concocted motor bicycles which they built themselves by attaching a motor to the back wheel of a regular bicycle. They rode them around Bedford during the Second World War, thereby saving gasoline.

One day Mom attempted to ride Daddy's motor bicycle down our challenging driveway. At the bottom of the drive, she went head first over the handle bars. Remarkably, she was unhurt; but that wasn't the state of the bicycle! Thankfully the war was almost over, and cars began to fill the streets of town once again. But Daddy's motor bicycle never did.

The Kitchen Table

The kitchen was small, but Mom and Dad liked to have their kitchen table placed in the center of the room. During the last years in their home, Daddy sat on the west side of the table and Mom on the east. Daddy's chair was close to the refrigerator door. Hardly a meal would go by without the need to take a forgotten item from the refrigerator. The routine was always the same. Mom would jump up and ask Daddy to move his chair over so she could open the refrigerator door. This inconvenient arrangement caused the same awkward scenario to be played out every day, at every meal.

After clearing the table and washing the dishes one day, I moved the kitchen table ever so slightly at an angle. The refrigerator door could be opened without Daddy getting up. That looked logical and sensible and would save lots of commotion, or so I thought. For the remainder of my visit, they left the kitchen table at an angle in the small room. But I noticed that when I returned a few months later, the kitchen table was again *square with the world.*

The Garbage Collectors

Long before there was a garbage disposal in the kitchen, there were animals in the back yard and barnyard that ate the leftovers. Mom had a habit of tossing the "scraps" over the back fence.

One day when my daughter, Cathy, and I were clearing the table for Mom, she asked for her Grandma's advice about some of the leftovers. Mom's answer was a classic: "Just throw 'em out back. Something will come along and eat 'em!"

Mom's Spin on Aging

One day Mom looked in the mirror and remarked, "Hmmm. I used to have yellow hair and white teeth. Now I've got white hair and yellow teeth."

Hidden Treasures

While Elaine and Jim and I were clearing out the house at *608 Randolph Street* for the last time, Elaine found a box that Mom had probably filled several years before. Placed carefully inside were two little blue and white satin dresses that she had made for Elaine and me and a knitted one piece romper that baby Jim had worn. Attached to these was Mom's hand-written note: "Kids, Here are some things that you can throw away if you want to. I just couldn't. Love, Mom"

Thank You, Honey

Daddy told me this precious and lasting memory he had of Mom. During her last months at home, they spent many hours in their recliner chairs in the living room, Daddy watching television or reading and Mom keeping her hands busy with needle and yarn projects.

She was experiencing the devastating effects of memory loss more each week, and she knew it. Every night when Mom was ready to go to bed, she would go to Daddy's chair, kiss him "Good Night" and say, "Thank you, honey, for doing so many things for me." Every night. They were married almost sixty-five years.

That's What I Call Trust

We never gave it much thought. Daddy had had an accident with an electric saw when he was much younger, and the fingers on his left hand weren't as long as those on the right hand. Just a matter of fact, to us kids. I didn't think there was anything that Daddy was unable to do.

Many years later, I learned that Mom was Dad's assistant in more tasks than I realized.

Daddy was affixing something up on a wall with a hammer and nail. He had some trouble holding the small nail tight enough with his left hand fingers. That's where Mom came in.

"Helen, can you hold this nail right there, while I pound it in?" I watched Mom hold a nail while Daddy pounded it into the wall. Now that's what I call complete trust-- trusting a guy with a hammer in his hand. The kind of trust that happens over many, many years of working side by side, knowing when to help and when to step back.

Partners through the Ages

Mom and Daddy were married almost sixty-five years when Mom went home to the Lord. During those many years as any couple, they changed and would redefine who they were and then go through another decade together. As the child that moved the greatest distance, I saw them least often. When they reached their eighties, I began to see them needing one another in new ways.

Daddy had an incredible memory. He knew who lived on every farm along any of the roads we traveled together. He would be able to tell me the name of the owners, how many children each family had, and where those kids had relocated. He could remember the number of acres on each family farm. He knew what each farmer raised. All of this was information he'd acquired during his forty-five year tenure working in the Bedford National Bank, serving as a pastor in many small communities in southwest Iowa and northwest Missouri, conducting around fourteen hundred funerals of people he knew, and being on the cemetery board for many years. He had memorized the locations of each family plot and which members of the family were already there. Daddy was blessed with a remarkable memory.

Unfortunately, Daddy developed arthritis in his back and shoulders and didn't move as quickly as Mom could. She began to take on some of the physical duties around the house and acreage. When Mom was eighty-three years old, she had a series of heart attacks. She survived that difficult chapter of her life, but her memory problems began shortly after that. She was able to stay at home until she was almost ninety-two years old, only because Daddy was giving her loving twenty-four hour care, with some assistance from family and friends.

On one of my last visits there, while both were still living at home, Daddy took me aside and said, "Honey, I've been blessed with my memory. Mother doesn't have that anymore. She relies on me for that." I listened and nodded.

Later the same day, Mom confided in me with this admission, "Honey, I can still get up out of a chair and walk across the room with no trouble, but Carl just moves so slow now. He needs me to get things done." I listened and nodded.

I realized how important each of them saw their own strengths in their relationship. They felt needed by the other one! They each thought they were the more fortunate one. Their diverse infirmities changed the relationship but cemented their lives in a new way. No wonder they were able to stay in their own home for so many years. But, as everything has an end, Mom and Dad's ability to stay together at 608 Randolph Street eventually came to an end also.

Chapter Eight

Growing Up In Bedford

A Lick and a Promise

It was Saturday morning. Mom would be multi-tasking in the kitchen when she would call to us. She spoke firmly and lovingly, "Girls, one or both of you, can you come here?"

Elaine and I would find Mom in the kitchen usually washing dishes at the corner sink. She had things all set up for us! A pan of soapy water and scrub brush or mop would be sitting on the floor by the back door. The dust mop for hardwood floors and dusting cloths for the furniture would be sitting beside the container of furniture polish. The vacuum was plugged in ready to go, and her Hamilton Beach mixer sat on the counter, primed and ready to create a dessert!

"Take your pick," she'd say.

The Saturday morning routine was predictable. Time to divide and conquer.

We learned that there were some tasks that we liked better than others. Elaine didn't like to vacuum. I did. I didn't like to scrub the kitchen and bathroom floors, so Elaine usually did those jobs. Later I discovered that she earned a Camp Fire Girl bead each and every time she scrubbed the floors! Smart kid, that girl!

We both liked to dust, so we took turns with that job. Mom would hand one of us the dusting cloth and furniture polish and say, "Just give it a lick and a promise." That always told us that Mom wasn't hosting one of her women's clubs any time soon.

When Mom got the house ready for club, the housecleaning tasks were anything but "a lick and a promise."

We were big on dessert at our house. We couldn't leave the table until we'd had dessert! So I'd usually elect to make a cake. (This was before Betty or Duncan or the chubby white doughboy came up with the idea of putting a cake mix in a box. Those didn't make their debut until the mid 1950s.) Sometimes I'd make a Jello salad; we ate lots of Jello!

I learned a lot from our Saturday morning routine:

Hard work never hurt anybody.

Share the work load whenever possible.

Enjoy the feeling of accomplishment when a task is completed.

Sometimes "a lick and a promise" is good enough!

The best part was something that we didn't realize at the time. We were making memories together.

Sunday School and Church

Our faith was an important part of our lives. It defined who we were, how we thought, what we did, and whom we counted among our inner circle of friends.

Mom's uncle, Rev. John Ashley Fitch, was a Presbyterian missionary in Chu Fou Shentung, China. I heard stories of his dangerous adventures in that far away country and his passion for the people there. His picture appeared in the Bedford Presbyterian Church Centennial program printed in 1957. That program was among the discoveries in the old house, that summer of 2003.

Rev. Jesse Herbert, a Circuit Rider and Charter Member of the First Methodist Church in Bedford, was my father's great grandfather. In an earlier era, John and Charles Wesley rode their horses going from congregation to congregation as they founded the Methodist Church. They were Circuit Riders too.

My first recollections of organized church began with the Baptist Church in Bedford, Iowa. Daddy began attending that church when he was in junior high school because his friends all went to the Baptist Church. So that's where they worshiped, even though Grandma Florence came from a family of Methodists. Our family never got "hung up" on different Protestant labels. We professed to be followers of Jesus Christ; the denomination just seemed like a label.

The great old Baptist hymns are still some of my favorites.

"Wonderful Words of Life"

"In the Sweet, By and By"

"Standing on the Promises"

"When the Roll is Called up Yonder, I'll be There"

At the Baptist Church, our family sat in the middle section near the back on the right aisle. Always. Grandma and Grandpa Cummings sat there too. I learned at an early age that people are creatures of habit. When I was quite small, I can remember standing up on the pew during the singing. From that vantage point I could check out the real vocalists. I had to be quiet during the sermon. I'd draw pictures or look around at the people and their kids. Sometimes I'd watch the sun play through the many colors of the elaborate stained glass windows on the east and west sides of the main sanctuary. I always felt welcome in a church.

In the summer everyone fanned themselves with the cardboard fans that had a flat wooden handle. Funeral homes advertised on one side and the other side displayed pictures of Jesus. This was an earlier version of air conditioning.

In the winter we'd keep our coats on if the furnace wasn't warming the big brick church. Near the doors were coat racks, if we dared remove our coats. Hats, coats and boots waited to be claimed by the rightful owner after the service.

At Christmas time there would be children's programs, and the audience always loved to see little kids go up on the stage and perform. Sometimes Santa would pay us a surprise visit and give each child a sack containing some hard candy and an orange. I was afraid of the big bearded fellow in the red suit; I hid my head behind my parents and cried. I still have a vivid memory of that frightening experience.

Daddy explained to me why I have early childhood memories of attending more than one church. Apparently, the folks attended the Baptist Church for a year and then the Methodist Church for a year. After several years of that routine, they decided to settle down at the Methodist Church.

That's where they attended regularly for the rest of their lives. Grandma and Grandpa Cummings continued to attend and keep their membership at the First Baptist Church in Bedford.

As kids growing up, we didn't know that there was anything else to do on Sunday morning except go to Sunday school and church. That was an important social and spiritual connection in the small towns of rural middle America. The rest of our day was also routine. After church Mom rushed home, changed into a housedress and made our favorite Sunday dinner: fried chicken, mashed potatoes and chicken gravy, Jello, vegetable (fresh or canned, depending on the season), and always a dessert.

Naps, reading the Sunday paper, or activities with extended family were the usual activities for Sunday afternoon. Mama would never dream of sewing on Sunday. I asked her why she was so strict about that. Her answer was, "Because my mother never sewed on Sunday." I imagine it was pretty hard on Mama, since she always needed to keep her hands involved in a project of some kind.

The Methodist Church in Bedford was the setting of lots of good times and fine memories:

- Saturday morning membership classes when I was eleven or twelve years old
- Sunday school classes in the basement on Sunday mornings
- Sitting with Daddy while Mama was the pianist for the Sunday service
- MYF (Methodist Youth Fellowship) for high school kids, on Sunday evenings
- Choir practice every Thursday evening, with Mildred Stacy serving as choir director as well as the organist

- Practicing the organ (when my feet finally touched the pedals) to prepare for a Sunday service
- Sitting in a full choir loft every Sunday and singing with a group of high school friends
- High School class led by J.S. Taylor and A. Elton Jensen

Maxine Freemyer taught my Sunday school class when I was about eight years old. She gave reassuring answers to our questions about heaven. I still recall the joyful gleam in her eyes as she carefully worded each answer.

Velma Shepherd and Alice Park were not only friends of our family but also were favorite Sunday school teachers, as well.

Mom and Daddy were MYF sponsors for several years. Mom was Sunday school superintendent for awhile as Daddy began his training period as a Methodist District Lay Pastor. While Mom played the piano for the children's opening exercises, Daddy would drive quite a distance on Sunday mornings to the various churches where he was a guest speaker or interim pastor. He followed in his great grandfather's footsteps. Rev. Jesse Herbert was a circuit rider; Daddy was a circuit driver. We three kids continued to attend the Methodist Church. Mom organized and led Vacation Bible School for a week each summer. The folks became involved in more church activities after I graduated from college and moved from Bedford. Daddy was the interim pastor for the Bedford Methodist Church twice. Church, definitely, held an important place in our lives.

Photo of Dad at the Baptist Church, Bedford, Iowa

The scripture on the stained glass window, behind Dad, reads:

"I have finished my course, I have kept the faith"

II Timothy 4:7

We sang many standard hymns at the Methodist Church but the real old gospel favorites of mine were sung at the Baptist Church. Sometimes I'd fill in when the organist at the Baptist Church was on vacation. I liked playing those hymns from the old brown hymnal. Being used to the louder, faster beat of the Methodists' music, I'd sometimes have to be reminded by Rev. Fred Cowles, Baptist minister, to slow it down and use the soft pedal on the organ.

Just like any relationship changes and grows, my relationship to my Savior, Jesus Christ, developed over time. Not rapidly, but over time. Through the valleys and peaks of life, and the times when I felt very much alone, I came to know the comfort and strength of His presence. When I thought I needed no other strength but my own, He waited patiently. Realizing that Christianity is not a religion, but is instead a relationship to my Creator, takes the whole issue of *works* out of the equation. Trying to grasp the full measure of His gifts of grace and love is something that I may never fully understand, this side of heaven. Borrowing the words of Apostle Paul in the last verse of the book of Second Corinthians sums up this relationship promised to believers: The **grace** of the Lord Jesus Christ, the **love** of God, and the **fellowship** of the Holy Spirit, be with you all. This fellowship is a comforting presence that can make prayer more like a continuing all-day conversation with Him and I don't have to say "Amen."

Being a charter member of Saddleback Community Church in Lake Forest, California, has been a very significant journey for me. Seeing the little community, begun in 1980, grow to one of the largest congregations in the United States has given me a first hand chance to see God at work. Pastor Rick and Kay Warren have been obedient to His voice. Imagine growing so large that we needed to rent the Angels' Stadium in Anaheim, California, to celebrate our twenty-fifth year! I wonder where our next celebration will be held.

"The grass withers, the flower fades; but the word of our God shall stand forever."   Isaiah 40:8

Number Please

It feels like the good ol' days when I watch a favorite old television show where Sheriff Andy Taylor picks up the phone and says, "Sarah, give me Thelma Lou."

We once had personal communication with a real voice just like that in Bedford, Iowa. A few friendly ladies sat at the switchboard all day and connected our voices on the telephone line. When lifting the receiver off of the old black wall phone, we could hear them respond with "Central" or "Operator" or "Number Please." A real person--a live voice--and we just took it for granted that telephone service would always provide that. How times have changed!

Back in the 1930s and 40s, folks were lucky to have one phone in the house. In farmhouses, a big wooden phone hung on the wall. A crank on the right side allowed the initiator to call another party with a certain coded ring. Two longs and a short; a short and three longs; three shorts and a long; these were typical numbers of folks in the country who shared a party line. On the left side of the phone was the receiver, which was lifted to the ear for listening. The black bell-shaped horn on the front of the wooden box took in the caller's voice. Shouting was often necessary if there was static on the line. And there usually was. Those old party lines were anything but private. News by this method traveled *fast*.

The first telephone that I remember at home hung on the wall above the desk in the dining room. Telephones came in one color: black. Our designated number was Red 190; Grandpa and Grandma Cummings' number was Black 101.

Later, the color was dropped and a letter was added at the end. 190M became our new number.

Some of the businesses downtown had only two digits. The Bedford National Bank was 71. We spoke our requested number into the phone, and the operator always responded with "Thank you." Service with a smile!

We didn't make long distance calls frequently. Calls made to Aunts and Uncles who lived eight miles west of town were considered long distance calls from Bedford.

"Operator, I'd like to make a long distance call." After the necessary information was given, there were several quiet minutes while a connection was made at the switchboard downtown. Long distance calls weren't cheap, so they were not made unless absolutely necessary.

Sheriff Andy Taylor and Deputy Barney Fife used a desk model on those early television shows. A free standing phone, it stood taller than the later desk models that cradled the receiver horizontally.

About the middle of the twentieth century, telephone numbers in cities began with a word prefix, such as Jefferson 3-2623. The rotary dial on the front of the telephone whirled around and slowly jerked back to the starting place between each number. If a caller was in a hurry, dialing the numbers 9 and 0 were anything but fast.

Changes happened quickly about this time. Word prefixes were changed into numbers and seven digit telephone numbers were the usual. Then our telephones, which we leased from the Bell Telephone Company, were recalled. We purchased our own telephones in a variety of styles and colors. We could install our own telephones since telephone jacks were built into most rooms of our homes. I thought it was really progressive when we could have a telephone in the kitchen, one in the bedroom end of the house, and maybe a third one on a desk somewhere in between.

Answering machines were slow to catch on at first. I think most folks liked to speak with a real person, but times were changing and people stayed home less often. The first answering machines were tape recorded, and when the tape was full, no more messages could be received. Later, these machines were updated to digital, and messages of unlimited length could be left.

Eventually, all telephone numbers were preceded by three digits called an area code. Calling direct to anyone, anywhere in the world became easier and not unusual, as our world seemed to become smaller.

Then other telephone companies got into the act, all claiming better service and lower prices than the next one.

Extension telephones were popular because they offered freedom of moving about while talking on the phone. Landline telephones weren't as popular because they required the caller to stay in one place, which made multi-tasking almost impossible. Well, not quite impossible. With a long expandable cord, moving around had greater possibilities. One day my friend asked me what I was doing while we were engaged in our usual long telephone visit. I told her that I was scrubbing the kitchen floor with my free hand.

Cellular telephones were, at first, used as emergency devices. They were not much smaller than an extension telephone. Now they are so small they can get lost inside a coin purse. Companies are now making cell phones especially for kids. What a market within the communications industry! Young people holding a cell phone to their ear wander through the aisles of super markets and department stores. They discuss the items on the shelves as they disclose their personal plans to the general listening crowd of shoppers. Hinges on being inconsiderate, in my opinion.

Today's generation of young people will remember growing up holding a tiny cell phone to their ear or wearing one attached over the ear. It seems they can't leave the house without one. With some features, they can even *see* the person they are talking to on a phone screen, as well as on a computer monitor. What could possibly be next? In the rapidly growing field of new communication discoveries, this paragraph will be outdated in a few days.

Most places of business have automated messages that spill out a menu a mile long, right after they tell you how important your call is to them. Frustration levels begin to mount. It's enough to make a customer search the yellow pages for a competitor, one who still pays a live person to answer the phone with a personal, friendly greeting.

I've seen the younger crowd carrying a small device inside the palm of their hand that programs their day, records anything they don't have time to write down, organizes their to-do list, makes telephone calls for them, gives them directions to a new address, in general, stores more information than a public library or a fat telephone book. They would probably get lost without it. I'm sure these small devices will get smaller and their capability will increase in just a matter of days. The newest electronic *essential* is called the *iPhone*. Recently hundreds of people stood in line waiting for a store to open so they could be among the first owners of the new *iPhone*.

Alexander Graham Bell didn't have any idea how his discovery would change the world. Like my Grandma Emma May O'Dell, I sometimes ask the same question, "I wonder if there will be as many changes in the next fifty years as there has been in the last fifty years?"

It staggers the imagination!

Wheels

I grew up with a tricycle and lots of room to ride. Inside the house was a complete circle joining one room to the next. Several acres of land gave us riding space outdoors. I spent hours riding my tricycle. Mom said that was how my legs became so *healthy*.

Elaine and I made believe that Randolph Street represented several states. We'd drive our tricycles on vacations from one state to the next. We had favorite spots under certain trees in Grandma and Grandpa's north yard as well as our own. We were allowed to cross Randolph Street and ride to Mrs. Johnson's or Mrs. Derrickson's *IF* we were really careful! We rode down to Harmon Miller's shop on the corner of Main and Randolph Street. But we couldn't ride across Main Street.

Then we went through our inventive stage. Elaine and I would find a pair of old rusty wheels on an axle lying around the barnyard and turn them into a jalopy. We'd take neighbor kids and all the pets for rides.

We used our red wagon to make pretend cars. I commissioned Elaine to sit backwards and run with her feet out the back, to propel us forward. She never complained, God love her. She was a good sport about that, and I know she did more than her share of the time acting as the motor.

We made many pretend trips and drives in the stationery old black '39 Ford. It sat in our driveway the entire trip, but in our imaginations we traveled the U.S.

When I was old enough to sit on Daddy's lap behind the wheel, he'd let me drive. I thought I was really grown up, even though I never let Daddy know that I knew that he never took his hands off the wheel. Seat belt requirements and children's car seats of today have changed all that.

Then Daddy and Mom bought us a bicycle, a two wheeler! Elaine and I took turns learning, falling off, and getting back on again and again. We rode along the terrace in the front yard while Mom watched us and timed us. After we learned to ride that bicycle, Daddy found a larger, used bicycle for me. It was a ghastly orange color. I intended to paint it one day, but I don't believe I ever did. It was nothing fancy, but it worked.

Elaine and I let our imaginations take us to distant places on our wheels. We rode out to the old cemetery west of town and thought we were in Outer Mongolia. We rode past the farms of Ralph Perkins, Tommy Park and Virgil Putnam on the gravel road which took us to Highway 2. We loved adventure, we loved to pretend, and we loved to ride our two-wheelers. And we always felt safe.

Daddy usually bought used cars. They are now called previously owned vehicles. Daddy liked to know the previous owner, how they drove the car, and how well they took care of it. The only new car he ever bought was a 1949 Ford. That car stayed in the family a long time. It took us on many family vacations.

Then the dreaded day arrived. Dreaded by parents but wonderfully liberating for teenagers. I took driver's education at school. Three students and one brave teacher would get into the driver's ed. car and take off for the football field or country roads. I learned that loose gravel can be dangerous, that driving just a little too fast can be exciting, and Iowa's old Highway 2 was a bit tricky because the curb along the edge could pull a car off the road. Other than a slight mishap on an icy road, I never was involved in an accident. My one bad driving experience happened at home before I even left the driveway.

This is how it happened. Every morning Daddy drove us to school on his way to the Bedford National Bank. I had had driver's training, but didn't yet have a learner's permit. I asked Daddy's permission to back the car out of the garage one morning. I had observed how Mom and Dad backed the car out of the garage. A sharp angled turn had to be made once out of the garage, so that the car could be turned to go headfirst down the long driveway. Behind the wheel of Daddy's '49 Ford, I put the car in reverse. Making the turn too soon, the left front end of the car met the left side of the garage. The load scraping noise brought Daddy to the south door of the house. I immediately got out of the car, felt incredible guilt, and told Daddy that I'd pay for the damage. He didn't say anything. He didn't show anger or compassion or humor. This was one time I wished he would scold me or take away privileges, or something. He stood by the south door and watched the shape of his car and the garage get changed (drastically and permanently), but he didn't show anger.

I remember that this happened on a Wednesday. Chapel was held in the high school auditorium every Wednesday morning. I remember praying that day for forgiveness and that a proper punishment would come my way. The punishment never came. I didn't have to pay for the damage, and Dad never brought up the subject again, except in his dry humor that came out often.

In a matter of weeks the dented fender was repaired and the garage was remedied as much as possible. It leaned to the South a bit more each year after that, always a reminder to me of how I had left my mark on that garage. Eventually, the building was taken down.

Now the sidewalk leads to nowhere. At least, that's the way most people would view it. But for me the sidewalk leads my mind to the day I messed up the family car and the little gray garage and learned about *grace* in the process.

Grace is one of the amazing gifts that Jesus made possible. It is unmerited, unearned, and undeserved. I was the receiver of a gift of grace.

Daddy showed me how it works.

The Good Ol' Days

The 40s and 50s in Bedford, Iowa

Small towns in the heartland of America bring up all kinds of nostalgia for me. Bedford, Iowa, was typical in many ways. The corner drug store, the five and dime, the courthouse located on a large block of green lawn, the ivy-covered Carnegie library, the park, the red brick two story buildings on Main Street, and the red brick streets; all of these are indicative of small towns that grew up along a railroad or river in the middle 1800s. The pioneers stayed and raised families. The next generation stayed, and so did the next. These patterns were still common in the 1940s and 1950s which, for me, were the good ol' days.

A small town with a population of about 2000 people, Bedford was a thriving little town. Farmers flocked to town on Saturday to do their *trading*. Saturday night was *the* big night when stores stayed open until 9:00 P.M. Ed and Opal Ahrens had the best seats in town when they sat on their balcony above their drug store to watch the activity below on Main Street. Inside their drug store, a kid could buy a ten cent cherry coke at the grand old polished wood, marble, mirrored soda fountain. Families from the country would come early enough to get a good parking space on Main Street where they would sit in their car and watch the passers-by and chat with friends. The Rialto Theatre was open every night of the week in addition to the Saturday matinee, a perfect place for kids who liked the cowboy and Indian Westerns, and other serials. The movies were called *picture shows*.

The bandstand which stood in the court yard was the place for band concerts on a Saturday night during the summer. Mama and Daddy played in the Bedford City Band in the bandstand in the late 20s and early 30s. The old bandstand was gone by the 1950s when Elaine and I became part of the trumpet and cornet section of our high school band. The band members set up folding chairs in the grass. A string of bright lights overhead enabled us to see our music. Swarms of bugs circled around the lights, and we were fair game for the biting mosquitoes. Folks sat in their cars, rolled down the windows to listen, and honked their car horns at the end of each number if they liked it.

Bedford still had a <u>Cudahy Packing Plant</u> in the 40s and 50s. Located at the east end of town, it was near the railroad track. There were still trains coming through town, mostly freight cars. For a while a lone passenger car would make the run to Creston or to Maryville. One winter weekend during an ice storm the only way for me to get back to Northwest Missouri State College in Maryville, Missouri, was to ride the train. For a few years, the *Bug* came through once a day, going north on one day and south the next. Then the trains died out all together, and the historic little red brick depot at the east end of Main Street was taken down.

Also at the east end of town was the <u>Bedford Sale Barn</u>. My Grandpa Clyde and Ivan Wells, our neighbor on Randolph Street, were auctioneers there. A sale was held every Saturday for the farmers with livestock ready to go to market.

The Parsons family owned the <u>locker plant</u>. It was located on Washington, one street south of Main Street. After the customer's animal was slaughtered, the meat was butchered to specification, wrapped, labeled, and placed in their rented locker drawer. The heavy door of the locker room would slam behind us, giving a feeling of being trapped inside a freezer, a really, *really* cold freezer. We'd shiver with cold waiting for Mama to unlock our drawer and take out several packages of meat. We kept a drawer at the locker plant for years. Eventually, Mom and Daddy purchased a large freezer that sat on our enclosed back porch.

Beside the locker plant was the <u>Wholesale Produce,</u> owned and operated by Wayne Harbour and his son Bob. Outside their door were heavy scales for weighing poultry, hides, fur, and anything else you wanted to trade.

"Uncle Wayne" as Daddy called him, had quite a reputation for his hundreds of letters of inquiry written to the Ripley's "Believe It or Not" column in the newspaper. His white suits in the summer and his new Cadillacs made him quite a visible and prominent character around town. His last illustrious career before retirement was that of Bedford's Postmaster.

E.I. Wilson and his son-in-law, Bill Hensch, owned <u>Wilson Hatchery</u> where Mom bought her baby chicks each and every spring.

<u>Cobb's Ice Cream</u>, locally owned and operated, had a plant in Bedford where we could buy the best ice cream in the country! Both of these establishments were in the east end of town, on Dodge Street, as I remember.

There were farm implement companies and auto dealers, as well as repair shops for both. Lumber companies, feed and seed companies, several plumbing and heating establishments, and a <u>Farmers Coop Elevator Co.</u> were thriving.

When Elaine and I were quite small, Mama would take us to the feed store where she purchased large cloth bags of feed for our animals. We got to help select the bag, not for its contents, but for the cloth fabric. Most little girls of that era had a few feed sack or flour sack fabric dresses.

Bedford had several service stations throughout town. The <u>Frosty Trete</u> did a booming business at the corner of Pearl and Dodge. Soft serve ice cream, sundaes with hot fudge topping, hamburgers, fries, and breaded pork tenderloins were just a few of their specialties.

Elaine and I liked to stop at the Conoco Gas Station on the corner of Main and Madison. It was the halfway point in our long walk from our piano lessons at Martha Dinwiddie's and Mildred Stacy's. They both lived on the last street on the east edge of town, and we lived on the last street at the west edge of town. On a hot summer day, we couldn't wait to stop at the Conoco station and pull a cold glass bottle of soda from the large red ice-filled tank. Using the bottle opener on the end of the tank, we'd open the bottles. My favorite flavor was grape; Elaine's was orange. Each one cost a dime. We'd finish our sodas at the station before continuing our long walk westward up Main Street to the top of the hill where Randolph Street begins.

Three main grocery stores were kept busy: the Hy-Vee, a new building on Madison across from the library; the Bedford Wholesale Fruit Company on Main Street; and Les and Mary Galey's Food Store at Court and Main.

Sometime during the 50s, a new ingredient was available in our grocery store. Its name was margarine. It was white in color, looked like shortening, and came in a box along with a foil packet of yellow food coloring. After the yellow coloring was mashed into the white stuff, it became the first butter substitute.

I have vague recollections of Sid Morris's Grocery Store. This was an earlier grocery store before the self-serve groceries, and if I remember correctly, it was on Main Street. Mama would make a grocery list at home. During the war, she took her ration books for sugar. When we entered through the front door, Mama would hand her list to Sid who collected the items and put them in a box at the counter. The customer waited near the front door. There was a bench just inside the store, and Mama would instruct Elaine and me to stay there until her shopping was done. Sid had an overweight bulldog in his store, a friendly dog that welcomed everyone. He always waddled over to greet us, and Elaine was unduly concerned that he might have a cold since his nose was always wet. A dog hanging out in a grocery store today would be cause for alarm! With the groceries boxed and ready to be carried to the customer's car, the financial transaction took place. The drawer of the large black and gold cash register would shoot open as bells rang, waiting for the clerk to slam it shut again. The box of groceries would be carried to the car. Since car doors were never locked and everyone knew everyone else's car, the box of groceries might be waiting for you when you reached your vehicle.

Having our own dairy animals, we seldom needed to purchase milk, cream, cottage cheese, or butter. I can still see that old metal pan of curds and whey sitting in the kitchen waiting to become cottage cheese. Mom's old butter churn now sits on a shelf among some of my antiques, along with her butter paddle and a wooden one-pound butter mold. Our livestock and chickens provided meat on the table. Everything in Mama's large summer vegetable garden was preserved by canning or freezing. Fruit trees and a grape arbor gave us fruit, which was also preserved. Sugar and flour, tea and coffee, seasonings and extracts, in addition to cleaning and laundry products, were some of the few necessities we had to purchase at the grocery store. We were pretty much self-sufficient, as most farm families were during the 40s and 50s.

Bedford customers kept several hardware and appliance stores in business and the two barber shops on Main Street had striped red, white, and blue barber poles at the front door, as I remember.

Two dentists, <u>Dr. Paschal, DDS, and Dr. Steward, DDS</u>, and two doctors, <u>Dr. Rimel, MD., and Dr. John Hardin, MD</u>, kept office hours daily except Sunday, and they would occasionally still make a house call. There are many stories of our doctors making impossible trips through the snow, rain, or mud when a baby was about to come into the world.

Main Street was scarcely four blocks long from east to west. Rarely would there be a vacant store or building. The cars of the 30s, 40s, and 50s seemed to fit the narrow downtown red brick streets. Main Street was a two way street with parking on both sides.

Bob Zeller and Rollie Livingston owned the <u>Zeller and Livingston Clothing Company</u>. It was a men's clothing store where Bob and Rollie, along with Delmar Fuller and Lute Taylor, wore a suit to work most of the time.

<u>Daisy's Dress Shoppe,</u> which later changed its name to <u>The Style Shop</u> under new ownership, was a classy place selling women's attire. <u>Thompson's Mercantile</u> still had the cashier lady who sat in her second story balcony, sending and receiving the customers' money. The money was placed in a container and a cord was pulled which shot the money cup along a wire to the balcony above. In short order, the cup would zip down the wire to the counter if the customer had any change coming. I was so fascinated by that thing, and I really thought I would like to have that lady's job some day, for the view, if nothing else. A huge roll of brown or white wrapping paper with a giant spool of string was a part of each station. Thompson's had ready-made clothing, shoes, and linens, as well as a notions and fabric department. Owned by members of the Thompson family, several of them worked in the store.

<u>The Garland Hotel</u> was a place for a nice Sunday dinner in the dining room. On occasion there was live entertainment while you ate. Mrs. Whitaker, Joe's mother, was the cook. Some of the single teachers that taught in the Bedford school system rented a room at the Garland for the school year. Several Bedford citizens made their home there. The polished wooden banister on the staircase and the tile floors in the lobby really impressed me, reminiscent of an earlier era.

Another hotel occupied the corner at Madison and Jefferson before the new Hy-Vee store was built there in the

50s. It was operated by the Giggly family where a very nice Sunday dinner could be enjoyed. Going out for dinner was seldom done back then. Most of the time, folks ate at home around the same table at the same time. It was the place for a family to connect, where important things were discussed.

Occasionally Elaine and I became engaged in hysterical giggling so that we couldn't eat. We had to be separated for a few minutes in different rooms before we were allowed to return to the table with a warning of "Act your age." I was never quite sure what "Act your age" *really* meant, since I was probably already doing that, which was precisely what got me into trouble in the first place. Or perhaps, our behavior was the reason we didn't eat out more often?

Bedford had one of the nicest jewelry stores in southwest Iowa. Caskey Jewelry had diamonds, watches and sterling silver as well as Lennox and Noritake China. Girls in high school and college would dream over the many patterns of china in the display case, hoping to choose one someday when they married. Before Caskeys owned the jewelry store, Mr. John Tracy was our jeweler in town.

A dear lady in Bedford, Rosa Hosman, adopted me as one of her children. Her birthday was the day before mine. Her birthday gift to me was a sterling silver spoon or fork or both, engraved with the year, elegantly wrapped from Caskey's store. Until I married and had a family of my own, Rosa didn't miss a year. After that I received a birthday card from her, signed in her distinctive, unique style of writing. She was a special lady who lived to see her one hundredth birthday. The sterling silver spoons and forks I received from her are treasures of lasting beauty, and I give them a place of honor in my home.

The *Bedford Times-Press* office was Rosa's work place. Other important people who worked there were Sid Morris, who wrote a sports column, Charles Hale and Donna Busby, who still live in Bedford, "Doc" McMillan, who was killed in a car accident when he was too young, and, of course, A.W. Hamblin, the editor of our home town paper. His weekly editorial was entitled, "Our Town." His daughter, Mary, wrote a column called "Scoop" which was the name of her small black and white terrier. She was also my Camp Fire Girls club leader when I was in fifth or sixth grade. After our meetings at Hamblin's home, we all piled into Mary's little car. She took each of us home. Scoop went along. Mary's sister Dodie wrote for *Life* magazine and lived in Europe most of the time. I still subscribe to the *Bedford Times Press* newspaper just to keep up with the latest news around town. That's another chapter yet to come.

Ed Ahrens came to Bedford in 1910. He bought the A.L. Bibbin's Drug Store which was located on the south side of Main Street across from the Bedford National Bank. Also in 1910, a new building was being built at the corner of Main and Central on the north side of Main Street. It was the Citizens State Bank. It had a corner entrance. Then in 1929 after the stock market crash, the Citizens State Bank closed. Ed purchased the bank building, changed the entrance to a south facing facade, and had the vault removed by James Salter's monument works. He remodeled the inside to include a grand old wooden, mirrored soda fountain on the east wall complete with tall stools at the counter. It was the hangout for people of all ages. Ed and Opal lived in the large front apartment above the drug store. The building changed ownership several times after Ed and Opal sold their business. The building burned on March 8, 1999.

This information about Ed Ahrens was left by my Dad on a typed sheet of paper which he inserted inside the Bedford Centennial book. Dad liked to document things and leave records for posterity. I'm passing this on to another generation.

In addition to Ahrens Drug store, there was the Bedford Rexall Drugs, also on Main Street, where friends gathered at the counter or in a booth for a coke or soda and waited for a prescription to be filled in the back of the store. Last, but not least, was <u>Rhoades store.</u> The Rhoades sisters, Hermie and Beryl, were not pharmacists like their father, but they kept the store open, selling paper products, books, and various things. The tall, wooden, glass-front cabinets still contained apothecary jars, reminding customers of a once-thriving pharmaceutical business. The musty odor of the store went out with every purchase. But they had merchandise that other stores didn't carry if the girls could find them. The two ladies lived together as many spinster sisters did in those days.

<u>Iowa Power and Light,</u> radio shops, <u>Bedford Battery, Western Auto, Katz Store, and Gambles</u> gave the town folks more opportunities to spend their money and support their town. The <u>Western Light and Telephone Company</u> employed a few ladies to run the switch board and connect our telephone calls. We still heard a real voice say, "Central," when we picked up the receiver to place a call.

The <u>Prugh</u> family had a very nice furniture, appliance, hardware store in a new building behind the new Hardin Theater. John Prugh and I started Kindergarten together. That building has since been taken down.

Pearly Blake and his daughter Lucille lived in the apartment above <u>Blake Radio and Appliance Store.</u> At one time this shop was named <u>Blake's Music.</u> Printed on their sheet music was "Blake's Music Store: Everything in Music." I liked to buy sheet music there. Our cousins, Bill and Ben, went there several times with Elaine and me. One day we saw a ukulele in the window. Asking our parents for the money, we returned to the store and bought the ukulele. After we paid for it, Mr. Blake asked us for a penny. Without giving his request a second thought, I handed him one penny. Once outside the store, Bill speculated that Mr. Blake's request for a penny seemed terribly unusual and that he either had a lot of nerve or must be quite poor. Bill came from Nebraska, a state that had no sales tax.

Cousins Bill and Ben knew that their parents, Blanche and Dale Rankin, had lived in Bedford for a short time before moving to Omaha. Uncle Dale had picked up a nickname while working in downtown Bedford. He was called "Preacher." But Ben didn't know that. When we went into one of Bedford's Main Street stores, a gentleman recognized Blanche and Dale's two sons and said, "Oh, you must be Preacher's boys." Ben's fast retort was, "No, I'm Blanche's boy."

The <u>Hamburger Inn</u> was a tiny little restaurant across from Dr. Paschal's dental office. Frances and Al owned it, cooked and waited on customers for decades, and always stayed lean and trim. Another café in town, The <u>Bedford Café</u>, was owned by the Pruitt family.

<u>The Skylark Café</u> was the gathering place for high school kids after the show at the <u>Rialto</u>. That's where I trained myself to drink coffee. It kept me awake lots of nights as I listened to the town clock in the courthouse strike one, two, and three A.M. Eventually, my body grew accustomed to the caffeine, I became a seasoned coffee drinker, and felt more grown up.

The little town had beauty shops, a shoe repair, and sometime in the 50s, Jim Jeters opened a dry cleaning business.

There were two spacious, well-kept, white frame funeral homes. One was owned by the Shum family which later became <u>Shum-Novinger</u> Funeral Home. Boyd Novinger married Wilma Shum and learned the trade from his father-in-law. The other funeral home was owned by the <u>Wetmore</u> family. Bud and Lucy Wetmore were not the first generation in that family business.

<u>Dr. T .E .Anderson</u> and his son <u>Don</u> were the veterinarians in town. Their office was on the south side of Main Street, at the east end. This was the business that my little brother Jim bought a few years after he graduated from

Iowa State University School of Veterinary Medicine and came back to his home town to live, work, and raise his family. With Dr. Don's influence and training Jim also became a horse owner. "Hawkeye" was the first name given to several generations of race horses owned by Dr. Don and my brother Jim. Jim continues to raise trotters for the harness races held throughout the state of Iowa.

Several insurance companies, the County Extension Office, the Farm Bureau office, and a Soil Conservation Office kept up with the times to serve the people of Bedford.

The two banks in town were both on Main Street, the State Savings Bank on the south side and the Bedford National Bank on the north side. The banks still had the black iron cages at each counter, separating the banker from the customer. Huge lobbies with marble floors and high ornate ceilings made the banks seem like museums. Large brass spittoons sat in several key locations in the lobby.

If I walked to town with friends after school, I could catch a ride home with Daddy after he *cashed out* at the Bedford National Bank. A light tap on the big front window would get his attention if the bank had already closed. He would unlock the front door of the bank and let me in. I'd wait in the lobby and think about the vast sum of money behind the heavy vault door and watch the manually-operated adding machines crank out numbers on long narrow strips of paper. When I was younger, Mr. W.E. Crum, Jr., President of the Bedford National Bank, would offer me a dime for an ice cream cone. Sometimes he'd walk to Ahrens Drug Store with me and make sure I got the flavor I wanted.

Daddy had great respect for his boss, Mr. Crum, and always addressed him by that name.

The Masonic Temple, a red brick building on Court Street, was the meeting place for the Masonic organizations in town. The I.O.O.F. Lodge #91 was on the other side of the street beside the old Fire Station. Odd Fellows, Rebekahs,

Masons, Eastern Star, and Rainbow were active organizations.

The volunteer fire department was made up of about 30 men. The cupola on top made it the tallest building on Court Street. The siren, or whistle, blew at 12 noon and 6 P.M. every day except Sunday. If the siren continued to crescendo several times, it was calling the volunteers to the station and alerting them to a fire.

The Carnegie Library

The red brick Carnegie Library, at the corner of Jefferson and Madison made a good impression to visitors traveling along Highway 148. Elementary age students were given a field trip through the library. High school students did research in the northeast corner room after school. Two stone fireplaces stood on the east and west walls. Any kid in town could get a library card, free of charge. Just walking up the many steps to the front door made a little kid feel important.

Across the street and east of the library stood the elegant old Taylor County Courthouse, its arches and architectural lines are reminiscent of the Romanesque style. It is affectionately called "the grand old lady with the white crown." The building was begun in 1892. My Grandma Florence remembered attending the dedication of the new building when she was only eleven years old. The four floors of offices and busy workers seemed extremely professional and impressive to me as a kid. The floor plan on the second floor was very much like the floor plan of the old grade school building, lots of space in the middle and a large room in each of the four corners. The clock in the tower keeps accurate time for the bell that chimes on the hour and every half hour.

The <u>statue</u> in the front of the building was built to honor the Civil War soldiers. Tall stately trees filled the court yard, and the Taylor County Sheriff's home with the adjoining jail house sat in the southeast corner of the square. For a time, the old bandstand occupied the slope between the sheriff's home and the courthouse.

Taylor County Courthouse

    The red brick streets of Bedford have undergone some careful maintenance after the city decided to restore them. There is a unique humming sound that automobile tires make on the red brick streets.

Left to right: Methodist Church, Taylor County Courthouse, Presbyterian Church in Bedford, Iowa

The churches were large, red brick buildings with steeples and gables. Each church had wooden pews, high ceilings, and a kitchen off of a fellowship hall in the basement. The bells in the towers could be heard all over town on a Sunday morning. Enormous stained glass windows were the standard design of their time, being built in the late 1800s or early 1900s. The <u>Methodist</u> and <u>Presbyterian</u> churches occupied the corners at the intersection of Madison and Pearl Streets. The <u>Christian Church</u> was on the corner of Pennsylvania and Jefferson and the <u>Baptist</u> church was on the corner of Main Street and West. The newest church building in town was the <u>Sacred Heart Catholic Church</u> on Main and Illinois Streets. There was an Interchurch Council in our community and on many occasions the pastors shared duties as several churches joined together for certain occasions. As I remember there were a few other smaller churches in Bedford during these two decades.

The <u>Taylor County Fairgrounds</u> were south of town where State Street begins to wander into the country on what is called the old St. Joe Road. Our favorite family event of the Taylor County Fair was the harness racing. The large white barn would be filled with horses waiting for their assigned time to race. The old grandstand was our family's favorite spot where we sat every summer, just down wind of the cigar smoker who came to every race, every summer, and sat in his favorite spot. I associated the smell of a cigar with harness racing for years. After each race, Dr. Anderson, Senior, up in the officials' tower, announced the *time of the mile*. I didn't understand what he was saying. It just sounded like a very long word with each syllable melting into the next. For years I associated that long strange word "timeofthemile" with harness races, dust blowing off the track, summer heat, and cigar smoke. Actually, with a measure of nostalgia thrown in, it's a sweet memory. Funny how time and age puts a twist on things.

The midway was exciting to a kid. I felt weak in the knees after the tilt-a-whirl ride and was afraid to look down when I rode the ferris wheel. We saw our share of gypsies that traveled with the carnival. They'd sometimes wander up to Randolph Street and ask if we'd *sell* them some live chickens.

Mama would hold on to us when we walked near a fortune teller's tent in the midway. She said we wouldn't want to go to those places. There were circus type acts, cotton candy on a stick, 4H buildings full of projects and animals in the stock pens. To a kid, it was a huge place of excitement that happened once a year, usually in July. And I felt sad after the midway rides had pulled up stakes and left town, leaving an empty space that seemed lonely the rest of the year.

The two <u>Bedford Public School buildings</u> sat beside each other, the old and the new. Both were constructed of red brick. I was impressed with the fire escapes that climbed to the third floor of the old grade school building. This was the high school building when my Mom and Dad attended Bedford High School in the 1920s.

There was a classroom in each corner of the large square building. In the 40s and 50s, grades three through six had classrooms on the second floor. Third grade was in the southwest corner and fourth grade in the southeast corner.

Below: The new high school building was built in 1926. My Dad once showed me a picture postcard of it. On the back he had recorded the total cost involved in building the high school. He liked to keep records of things like that. He was the secretary of the school board for twenty-five years.

My fourth grade teacher was Miss Dory. She was also my Aunt Blanche's fourth grade teacher. Teacher longevity was common then, especially among the single female teachers. Fifth grade was held in the northeast corner and sixth grade in the northwest corner on the second floor.

The junior high grades of seven and eight were upstairs on the third floor. Each classroom had a coat room where lunches, baseball equipment, coats, boots, umbrellas and other necessary accoutrements were safely stored.

Above: Formerly the High School built in 1904, it was where I went to grades three through eight. Mom and Dad graduated from high school in this building in 1924 and 1925 respectively.

Mr. Tucker was our custodian. He was a real friendly gentleman who sat in the chair on the second floor between the fifth and sixth grade rooms. When it was time to ring the school bell, he pulled the long heavy rope that disappeared through the ceiling to the bell tower above. We ran inside when that bell summoned us to start the school day in the morning, after lunch, and at the end of every recess. The *flat* was a large, level area east of the old building. It was used for games, marching band practice, gym classes, and sports practices. A jungle gym stood east of the flag pole. Every student attended a flag ceremony around the flagpole on the first day of school.

Kindergarten, first, and second grades were on first floor of the new building. They seemed like huge rooms to a kid, but upon seeing those rooms forty years later, I was amazed that twenty children would fit into those small classrooms. Miss Alice Hale gave many children their first experiences in Kindergarten.

Daddy took me to my first day of kindergarten in 1944.

East of town was the football field where high school football games were played and well attended on Friday nights. The Bedford High School marching band played the national anthem before the game, performed at half-time, and played fight tunes to liven up the cheering fans in the pep club. I played the *charge* on my little gold cornet before each kick off. The scene wasn't complete if Coach Shupe wasn't pacing up and down the field, fiercely chewing his gum, and yelling out plays and shouting encouragements or *whatevers* to his team.

It seemed like the low-lying football field was the dampest, coldest spot in town when the fall evenings took on a definite feel of the approaching winter. In anticipation of those cold evenings, Mama often made a large pot of cream of potato soup for Friday night supper. A bowl of cream of potato soup for supper on a chilly evening is still just right.

A new football field has been relocated west of town, and in its previous location, new ball diamonds have been established in honor of a beloved coach, Gene Hannon, and baseball fan and supporter, Harold Guenther.

Seven cheerleaders wore their purple and white uniforms, each with a letter on their backs, spelling B E D F O R D. Cousin Louise and little sister Elaine were both bouncing cheerleaders during their high school years. During basketball season their uniforms changed but the cheers were the same, as the basketball gymnasium at the high school was filled with Bedfordites, the townspeople who supported their team.

The school colors are no longer purple and white. Imagine that!

The low, flat grounds east of the football field became baseball diamonds in the spring and summer. In the winter the area was flooded to create an ice rink. This was also an area near the 102 River that was frequently flooded during heavy rains. The <u>water works plant</u> was just east of the baseball fields, a place most kids visited on a field trip, sometime in elementary school.

<u>Minstrel shows</u> were a big event for the community and were held in the Bedford High School Auditorium. The entire community took part in these, usually sponsored by the <u>Lions Club</u>. The large choir, directed and accompanied by Mildred Stacy, sounded very professional. Our family always went to those performances when I was a kid, as well as most of the Junior and Senior High School plays. Daddy was on the school board for twenty-five years and liked to be a part of school events as often as possible. In my high school years, which were from 1953 to 1957, I played a part in the junior and senior plays, but the minstrel shows were discontinued by then. The Civil Rights Movement was more important than minstrel shows in the 1950s.

The town of Bedford celebrated its <u>centennial in 1953.</u> Mayor Lester Round made a proclamation to all of the male citizens of shaving age to let their facial hair grow. Beards and mustaches on the men seemed to be the norm that summer. Daddy grew a beard. Men, women, and children wore colonial-style clothing. Mom sewed long colonial dresses for Elaine and me and herself. There were events for kids and adults such as horse shows, antique displays, dinners, square dances, a parade, and a centennial pageant at the fair ground.

On the evening of the pageant, an Iowa cloudburst sent people running for shelter. Carloads of people streamed out of the parking lot at the fairground, some never to return for the pageant. Unfortunately, Elaine and I had a ride with a driver who was unwilling to return to the fairgrounds. We have always regretted that. We were supposed to march with the high school band during one of the scenes in the Centennial skit. Can't imagine how they got along without us! Daddy gave his famous William Jennings Bryan speech as part of the historical pageant.

The day after the official centennial celebration ended, men began to shave off their beards.

The <u>Lake of Three Fires,</u> located a few miles northeast of Bedford is a state park. It was built by the CCC during President Franklin Roosevelt's administration. The beach area would be swarming with swimmers and sunbathers on weekends. There was a lifeguard on duty, and the snack bar was open. It was *the* place to be on a Sunday afternoon after church and after the family dinner at noon. Swimming lessons were given during the week in the summertime. There was a boat dock where rowboats could be rented by the hour. My friends and I explored every cove along the far edge of the lake from a rowboat. Picnic areas and shelter houses dotted the grounds. A few cabins sat on the edge of the lake's northern end, where families rented a rustic cabin by the week. Several times groups of my high school and college friends held slumber parties in a cabin at the Lake of Three Fires. When I was a Camp Fire Girl in fifth grade, my troop walked around the lake, which was a real accomplishment for a bunch of ten and eleven year olds. At least, we thought so. Lots of picnics and family reunions took place at the lake every Sunday during the summer. A group had to go early to stake out a claim for a shelter house or table before the crowds arrived.

In more recent years, the Fourth of July fireworks have been displayed over the Lake of Three Fires as viewers watch from their lawn chairs, fighting off the mosquitoes and hoping that the rain waits until the light show is finished.

<u>Bibbins Park</u>, at the northwest corner of town, was a place for kids to play on the slides and swings and for families to gather for picnics. Tennis courts were lit up for night playing. A narrow dirt road curled around the huge trees beside the croquet court and circled back over a narrow bridge. When I was a kid, the members of the <u>American</u>

Legion Post met in a building hidden away at the back end of Bibbins Park.

Bedford had two cemeteries. The Bedford City Cemetery was just west of town, and Fairview Cemetery sat at the south edge of town with the mausoleum at the east edge of it. Each Memorial Day, our high school band marched from the Courthouse or the high school up to Fairview Cemetery at the end of Orchard Street. The muffled and slower cadence began as we entered the gates of the cemetery. The band members stood at attention in formation during the ceremony. Every year, without fail, one or two of the band members would faint dead away and lie in a heap on the ground. The march along with the humidity and the standing seemed too much for some. In short order they came to and made their way to a bench or a car. Elaine and I did our share of playing the mournful "Taps" on our little gold cornets. One of us would wander off some distance from the crowd and play the *echo* which was last on the program.

There were other older cemeteries dotting the countryside, some in dire need of attention. On one of my Camp Fire excursions, we thought we had discovered an ancient cemetery east of town. The headstones were broken and lying on the ground, looking damaged and deserted. That was an exciting, somewhat scary experience for a group of ten year old girls, who compared the experience to the stories we loved to read in the *Nancy Drew* mystery book series.

Bedford's earlier water tower looked like a gigantic white silo, with a single ladder scaling its way to the top. This water tower, sometimes called the standpipe, was located on the east side of south Randolph Street. Classmates, Bill and Ron Reed, along with their sister, Agatha, and parents, Roy and Iola, lived directly across the street from the old water tower. The tower was taken down in 1952. When it was demolished, it was left lying on the ground for weeks. Being winter time, some of the water left inside was frozen in large chunks, large enough to sit upon. My friends and I bravely entered the dark, cold, horizontal tube, and sat on the ice chairs and listened to our voices echo through the old water tower.

A newer water tower replaced the old sometime in the early 50s. That tower still stands on Highway 148 north of town.

A mile or so beyond the new water tower on the highway is the nine hole <u>golf course</u> and <u>country club</u>. As a beginning golfer, I sank a thirty foot putt on the seventh hole, obviously a lucky accident. A bar and restaurant has been a part of the country club at various times through the years.

One of my favorite stores on Main Street was the <u>S&G Store.</u> This was similar to Ben Franklin chains and other Five and Dime Stores. The toy section in the back was a great place for a little kid to spend some time and money. When we were little, Elaine and I received a modest allowance and loved to spend some of it at our favorite store. Much later, another chain called Places came to town and the S&G had to go.

The good ol' days hold memories of these things:

- Birthday parties at the homes of my friends as well as my own
- Vacation Bible school in the summers
- Riding a bicycle across town after dark and feeling safe
- Listening to favorite Saturday morning radio programs: Smilin' Ed and Archie Andrews
- Warm long stockings or slacks under my dress in the winter
- Summertime water fights with a hose in the back yard

- Hot lunches at school complete with a thick slice of homemade bread
- Tutti Fruit Bubble Gum contests
- Roller skating to my Saturday morning tap dance lessons with friends and wearing my skate key on a ribbon around my neck
- Jumping rope at recess until my sides ached
- Climbing on the jungle gym on the *flat* at school
- Waiting for the chocolate cake to come out of the oven and knowing that Mama never made us wait until it cooled before the first bite
- Fixing a playing card to the spokes of my bicycle wheels with a clothespin.
- Playing in the front yard on summer nights until 9 P.M.
- Dr. Hardin's penicillin shots in the fanny and/or a bottle of red medicine, for just about every ailment under the sun
- Sledding down Main Street or Court Street in the winter
- Exchanging all of the *Nancy Drew* mystery books with my junior high school friends until we had read all of them
- Listening to music on Monday night radio
- Leaving the keys in our cars and knowing everybody else did too
- Going to the drive-in movies with a group of girl friends and sitting on the hood of the car. One time we dented it badly, but Daddy didn't punish me for it

- Double dating at the skating rink in Clarinda or Lenox, or the bowling alley in Maryville or the movies
- The night in 1955 when the old Rialto theater and surrounding buildings burned
- Listening to Elaine and her group of friends tell about their Halloween night tricks (things I would never think of doing!)
- Pep rallies before the junior high and high school football games
- Hi-Fi (high fidelity) record players, 78 and 45 rpm records.
- Playing hide and seek in our cars, in the alleys, and dark streets
- Sock hops in the gymnasium, poodle skirts, bobby socks, and saddle shoes
- Several layers of stiff starched petticoats beneath our full circle skirts
- Dance lessons with high school friends and learning the jitterbug to the latest hit, "Rock Around the Clock"
- Going to chapel every Wednesday morning in the high school auditorium
- Eating dinner from a TV tray while we watched *snow* on our first television set
- Keeping the car radio set on WHB, Kansas City, Missouri.
- Expressions like "See 'ya later, Alligator" and "After while, Crocodile."

 I never had to move to another town or even to another house. I have yet to live in any one house as long as

I lived at 608 Randolph Street. I felt sympathy for new students in class who had been uprooted and had to make new friends, even as my own two children have had to do several times. My upbringing was as stable as they come.

A dozen classmates and I started to kindergarten in the same room in 1944 and graduated from Bedford High School together on the same night in 1957. We knew the names of each other's parents, their brothers and sisters, other relatives in town, and even the names of their family pets. We knew who lived in almost every house on every street in town and what kind of a car each family owned. Whether that was stability or lack of privacy or somewhere in between is a matter of speculation; that's just the way I remember it.

At the time I didn't appreciate the humble, safe surroundings of our small town. Seeing the way the world has changed since then makes me realize how lucky we were. Even when the world was at war, we felt safe and sheltered from the craziness going on in other continents.

I knew that there was a big world outside of Bedford, Iowa, and I was anxious to experience it.

There is an old saying that goes like this:

"Parents can give their children two things--roots and wings."

Mom and Daddy gave us both.

Everything changes, even small towns. When I listen to the *oldies,* the tunes that were popular when I was growing up, I succumb to a nostalgic journey back to a little town in Iowa during the 40s and 50s. Those years will always be the good ol' days to me.

The view from the top of the Taylor County Courthouse

Photos by Carolyn with the exception of the two school building pictures.

Mother's Accident

When Mom made a promise to someone, she kept that promise, no matter what.

The women at the Methodist Church planned their spring luncheon. Mom promised that she'd contribute a homemade cake. She also promised that she would pick up another cake from a member who lived east of Bedford.

On her way back to town with both cakes in the front seat beside her, the camper truck that she was driving hit some lose gravel and landed in the ditch...on its side. Mom's foot landed in one of the cakes, but she was determined to deliver as promised. Somehow she crawled out of the window on the driver's side, which was on the top of the camper. With the cakes in both hands, she managed to hitch a ride with a gravel truck to the nearest farmhouse. It was the home of Homer Horning. Mrs. Horning agreed to give Mom a lift into town after she'd heard her story.

Just as Mrs. Horning was dropping off Mom at the church, Daddy arrived to join her for lunch. He asked, "What happened?" to which Mom skirted the issue and vaguely answered, "Oh, that's Mrs. Horning." When Daddy asked about the camper, Mom answered, "Oh, the camper? (pause) Why, it's out by Homer Horning's place."

Mom delivered her cakes to the kitchen as promised. She offered a kind of apology for the condition of the cake that had a footprint in it!

As they ate lunch together, Daddy began to piece together bits of truth, and Mom began to feel pain in her ankle, foot, and back. Because she felt so sad about wrecking the camper, she stayed in denial about the physical damage that her body had sustained.

But the pain didn't go away. By the next morning Mom was ready to go to the hospital. Aunt Neva joined her sister for the trip to the hospital.

At the Clarinda hospital, X rays revealed a fractured vertebra and a broken bone in her right foot (the foot that landed in the cake). Unfortunately, Mom experienced a lot of pain during the week in the hospital.

Daddy never liked to be the bearer of bad news unless it was absolutely necessary. He sat down at his favorite Underwood manual typewriter and composed a letter to us kids.

The letter began, "I take this means of advising you of Mother's accident last Thursday."

Three days later I received Daddy's letter. I read the first sentence, and without finishing the letter, I picked up the phone and called Daddy for more information. He filled in the blanks, told me Mom would like a call, and I took down the phone number. My family and I lived in Hopkins, Minnesota, and going home to Bedford at that time was not likely.

Elaine and Dick lived in northern Iowa. She got her letter the same day I received mine. She called me immediately after she had talked to Daddy. She was furious. Not only was she unhappy that Daddy had written to us instead of calling us, but she was fuming because she got a carbon copy of my letter. She said, "My letter has blue letters like a carbon. Did I get the carbon copy?" She was one upset little sister.

Jim and Rosalyn lived in Nebraska. Elaine and I just assumed that Jim probably got a letter as well. Many years later, Jim confessed that Daddy had informed him of Mother's accident by way of a phone call, not a letter. Oh well, what the heck! The folks really wanted a son, and they waited a long time for Jim!

Mom wore a back brace for a few months and tried to stay off the foot as much as possible. These things didn't seem to slow her down too much. She fixed a family dinner a few weeks later when we were all home at the same time. Her recovery was miraculous.

When Mom made a promise, she delivered, no matter what!

Radio and Television

I don't ever remember waking up and going downstairs to the kitchen without hearing the sound of the radio playing. Mom and Daddy listened to KMA from Shenandoah, Iowa, every morning—*every morning*! Sometimes during the day they might switch to WHO in Des Moines, Iowa. The farm reports, the homemaker's programs, the news reports were heard daily. *Don McNeil's Breakfast Club* was a favorite morning program, and sometimes the harmony of the Blackwood Brothers' quartet would fill the kitchen. On Saturday night when Mom filled the bathtub with a warm bubble bath for Elaine and me, the radio sounds of the *Saturday Night Barn Dance Frolic* could be heard coming from the kitchen radio.

The brown table model radio always sat in or near the north window of the kitchen. Right outside the window was the thermometer so a person could get a quick temperature reading as the radio warmed up. It hummed for awhile before sending a signal over the air waves. If a thunder and lightning storm was approaching, static would replace the program.

We were a four radio family in the 1940s; plus I think we had one in the old car that seemed to specialize in playing static.

Daddy's big wooden floor model radio sat beside his big brown chair in the living room. It was made by General Electric Company. Its new home is with Elaine now. It still works today, although Elaine and Dick don't spend much time sitting around it listening to its every sound! Not like folks did in the 1940s. Radio was a great invention that brought the country into its first instant communication system from coast to coast.

The third radio was in Mom and Daddy's bedroom and the fourth one sat on a night table in the bedroom that I shared with Elaine. The best morning for radio was Saturday. Our favorite program was *Archie Andrews,* who with his friends Jughead, Betty, and Veronica, always made some kind of trouble that filled the half hour show. Smilin' Ed McConnoll with his friend, Froggie, came on later. If we didn't have to get up at a certain time, we could be lazy for a whole hour being entertained by our radio.

Around supper time during preparation or dish washing, the kitchen radio brought us entertaining shows like *Fiber McGee and Molly, Father Knows Best, One Man's Family, Henry Aldrich, and Ozzie and Harriet.*

Some of these shows were brought to us by the JELLO commercials.

"The big red letters stand for the JELLO family,

Oh! The big red letters stand for the JELLO family,

That's JELLO, yum, yum, yum,

JELLO pudding, yum, yum, yum,

JELLO tap-i-o-ca pudding, yes sireeeee!"

At lunch time the commercials tried to sell listeners on the wonders of soap, for cleaning, for clothes, for the skin. And it was not unusual to hear several musical commercials from a feed company.

"Feed your hogs Nutrena,

NU-TRENA,

The best feed that money can buy."

The sounds of yesteryear sometimes refuse to go away.

Old time radio brought us some of the best music ever carried over the air waves...the big bands, the swing era, sounds of the Dorsey Brothers and Glen Miller. Live music that came from dance floors all across the country filled the homes of America every evening. *The Firestone Hour* and *The Railroad Hour* on Monday evenings brought popular music as well as classics into our homes.

When I began driving the folk's 1949 Ford, I left the radio station set on WHB Kansas City, Missouri. Music filled the car with the popular sounds of the 50s. Mom didn't appreciate "that loud old music" and switched quickly to her favorites. It wasn't easy being the oldest. Our parents didn't exactly embrace the new rock and roll sounds. Not then. But by the time Jim's band practiced in the living room, they must have either accepted it or were made deaf because of it.

There were very few families in Bedford, Iowa, who owned a television set before 1950. By the mid 50s most families had a T.V. set. Daddy came home with a black and white Emerson television set in January of 1954. The screen was circular, and the housing was real wood. It sat at the end of the long living room against the west wall. That site was the location for every subsequent television set that the folks owned.

We were amazed at the snowy images on the screen. There was a Circus show that caught the attention of children and adults alike. Some of our favorite sitcoms were *Our Miss Brooks* with Eve Arden, *Ozzie and Harriet, My Little Margie, Red Skelton, The Jack Benny Show, Burns and Allen*, and Mom's favorite, *I Love Lucy*. Before we had a television set, we would accept every invitation from Ed and Opal Ahrens to watch Lucy on Monday nights with them.

We liked to watch *This is Your Life,* a show that would catch a celebrity by surprise as their life was reviewed before a television audience of thousands. *The Web* and *Dragnet* were favorite weekly programs. *Strike It Rich* was a forerunner of today's game shows. Every Saturday night we watched *Your Hit Parade* and Daddy's favorite, *Gunsmoke*. These shows were brought to viewers by tobacco companies, selling cigarettes by using jingles and phrases that stayed with the viewer, like "Throat Hot? Smoke Kools," "I'd Walk a Mile for a Camel" and little Johnny in his bell hop uniform yelling out, "Call for Philip Mor-ris."

Personalities like Arthur Godfrey, Groucho Marx, Milton Berle, and Art Linkletter earned their fame as television pioneers. Eventually, full length movies came to television which changed the theater-going habits of many Americans.

Today more information goes out from one radio station or television channel in one hour than used to hit the air waves in a day. Keeping up with the many changes in communications is a full time job.

I'm glad I'm retired.

Mother was a Quilter

A quote from Teresa Palma Acosta's poem, "My Mother Pieced Quilts," describes my mother's quilts as well as her heart:

> "...stretched out they lay
> armed / ready/ shouting/ celebrating
> knotted with love
> the quilts sing on"

Mom loved to have a quilt in the frame. It meant that she always had a project, something to work on, anything to keep her hands creatively occupied. She usually sewed the fabric pieces together with her sewing machine. But the quilted designs, carefully drawn in place along the borders and integrated into the pattern, were ALWAYS quilted by hand.

She would enlist Daddy's help when it was time to lay the batting between the quilt top and the lining. She'd spread out the lining, right side down on the living room floor. Daddy helped her spread the batting over the lining. The quilt top was carefully placed on next, so that each corner matched. Daddy handed the pins to Mom, one at a time, as she attached the three layers together. It took both of them to wrap this evenly around the long wooden board of the quilting frame. The frame kept the quilt tightly stretched-ready for Mom's delicate handmade quilting stitches... seven tiny stitches on the needle, sometimes more. She stopped only to prepare a meal for herself and Daddy. Into the night she worked, long after Daddy had fallen asleep in his favorite recliner chair.

Most of our quilts were made by Mom after she turned eighty years old. I believe that mine was the first one of many that she made for her children and grandchildren. In one corner of my quilt, she stitched the year: *1986.* In another corner she stitched the word *Mother.* What a treasure!

Each of us chose the colors and the quilt pattern we wanted for our own. Mine is raspberry and cream. The pattern is the LeMoyne star (an eight pointed star). Lined up and down the quilt are thirty of these complicated blocks.

The real art of the quilting process is not only in the pattern and the fabric choices. It is also in the meticulous, consistent, handmade stitches that superimpose another work of art over the fabric design. Mom was an expert at this.

Elaine and Jim received their quilts made by Mom, the year after mine was completed. Then, in a very ambitious moment, Mom decided to make a quilt for each grandchild-- from the oldest to the youngest. Eventually, she could complete one of these works of art in four or five months. She made eight double/queen size quilts for all of her grandchildren: Cathy, Steve, Peggy, Susan, Matt, Carla, Ben, and Jeff.

As Mom stitched her love and prayers into each quilt, I imagine that she replayed memories of each child and grandchild. I bought a leather thimble for her finger, the one that worked underneath the quilt and directed the needle in and out through the cloth. She tried it, but concluded that her stitches looked better without the thimble. So with every tiny stitch she would prick her finger.

After Mom had finished eleven quilts, Daddy reminded her that she had not yet made one for him. That was the twelfth quilt that Mom completed. After that she made several others, some were donated to the church or to auctions as fundraisers. When one of her quilts was auctioned off for one hundred dollars, Mom was astounded. Her words were, "Why, forever more. You don't mean it."

Mom told me once that she didn't want to leave this earth with a quilt half-finished. That would explain the relentless, driving force that kept her working long hours without a break. She developed back pain from sitting too long at the quilting frame. Her shoulders became more rounded, but she continued to quilt as long as she could.

As Mom began to forget some of her knowledge of sewing and quilting, we would send smaller projects for her to do. She hand-quilted many crib size quilts and pillow tops. She would finish them in record time.

Before Mom and Daddy were married, Mom made a beautiful quilt for her hope chest. It was the star pattern, with pastel shades of gold and yellow blended together. There were probably other hands involved in its completion, but she had it done before she married. It was the custom of young maidens to have completed a quilt before she was twenty-one, lest she never marry. Another tradition states that if a young girl slept under a new quilt, she would dream of the boy she was going to marry.

Mama's long hours of work have left us with many treasures; each one is a loved and valuable work of art.

"Knotted with love, the quilts sing on."

The Fourth of July

The best place to really celebrate a patriotic and leisurely Fourth of July is *not* in the heart of Times Square in New York City, nor on Disneyland's Main Street in California, nor any other big, overpopulated and popular stage in America. I'd prefer a Fourth of July parade down the middle of Main Street in Bedford, Iowa, or any other small town in the heart of the U.S.A.

There is a different spirit among the folks in a small town, folks who know each other, grew up together, and watched generations of families walk across the stage of life. Real people. Long-lasting friendships. What the parades lack in elaborate floats is more than balanced by the show of effort and creativity when a tractor pulls a flatbed along the parade route with the winning float in tow. And little kids sitting on the curbs scramble for the candy being thrown from the floats. Small communities take the opportunity of turning an occasion into a celebration!

Little kids put a leash and a clown collar on their dog, babies ride in a wagon or buggy decorated with patriotic details, small sized bicycles with tiny riders make a memory they will never forget, as they travel on the red brick streets of Bedford. Supportive parents, grandparents, and friends clap and cheer as young ones parade before them. It is so simple and honest; no one can do it wrong. I like the leisurely pace of both the parade and the crowd. The crowd doesn't begin to show up with their lawn chairs much before 10 A.M. If the parade gets a late start, the parade can start at 10:30 as well as 10:00, and no one grumbles about keeping to a schedule. The beans and corn in the fields won't need any attention for several weeks.

Admittedly, there have been times when this life in a small town puts me in a kind of time warp, and I find it difficult to feel the energy of the town. Eventually, I fall into the groove of the slower rhythm of the place I still call home.

One year I watched the aging members of the color guard laboriously moving along at the head of the Fourth of July parade. People stood. Hats were removed. A quiet reverence settled over the crowd. A few seconds later someone in the crowd yelled to a member of the color guard. "Hey, Harve. Lookin' good."

Before Harve could respond in kind, another member of the color guard spoke up, "Harve always looks good." On they marched; a stunned silence fell over the crowd. A few snickers were heard. Maybe no one knew what to say. Or maybe that's just the rhythm of the life in this small community in southwest Iowa. One wouldn't see that in Times Square or Disneyland.

By the way, Harve was the name used in this account; I don't remember his real name.

As a child I stood with Mom, my little sister and brother as we watched the parade travel down Main Street. Daddy was often riding with the Saddle Club or elsewhere in the parade. Then sometime before we were in junior high, my sister and I became members of the high school marching band. It was the only band in town, and since every parade needs a band, we marched.

One year Daddy was the Grand Marshall in the Bedford parade! On several occasions, Dad and Mom drove a Studebaker in the parade.

Mom and Dad in a Studebaker in the Fourth of July parade. The Ahrens building is in the background, on the left

Much later, in their twilight years, I helped my parents settle into a lawn chair somewhere along the parade route.

I liked being in Bedford for the Fourth of July. It's a good time for a small town girl to return to her roots, entertain symptoms of nostalgia, recall memories, and make new ones.

These are just some of my favorite memories of a Fourth of July in Bedford:

- Reconnecting with old friends and alumni
- Hot, humid weather-- perhaps a surprise rain
- A horse show in the afternoon at the fairgrounds, where Daddy, Uncle Herman, and sometimes, Cousin Keith, and little brother Jim took part in the races
- A picnic of corn on the cob, or *roasting ears*, Mama's famous fried chicken, and homemade ice cream, in the hand-cranked freezer, of course.

- In later years, Jim's hamburgers cooking on the grill outside on the new patio
- Fireworks, legal or otherwise
- Being with family, sharing stories and memories
- Fireworks over the Lake of Three Fires State Park after dark

One year an electrical storm came up suddenly after only a few of the fireworks had been sent up. It was a downpour. Hundreds of people dashed to their cars, while the fire department lit off the remainder of the fireworks in one gigantic explosion of color and sound. As a steady stream of cars made their way out of the state park onto the road leading into town, nature's lightning show flashed across the sky. No one could be disappointed at the demise of the fireworks display. A Midwestern thunder and lightning storm is a necessary part of life in the heartland. I still miss them.

That night in my old upstairs bedroom with the south window slightly opened, I scooted the white antique iron bed closer to the window. I tried to sleep with one eye closed, while the other eye caught the patterns of light across the sky. It was too good to miss. I listened to the fading rumble of the thunder as the storm trailed off into the distant sky.

No doubt about it, there's nothing that compares with a Midwestern thunder and lightning storm, especially if it comes on the heels of a small town Fourth of July parade and a gathering of family and friends.

Did Mama Ever Sit Down?

"I wonder what she does in there?" Daddy would lament as we waited in the car for Mom. The three of us kids would be sitting in our usual places in the car, waiting, with our eyes peeled on the south door, knowing that at any moment Mom would come exploding out the door on the run. Many years and two children later, I understand and appreciate all the things that Mom did after she got the kids ready to go someplace. She would put on her make-up, run a comb through her hair, finish a quick pre-prep of the next meal, find her purse and coat, and run for the door. Mom didn't have a slow gear.

Daddy often told about his wedding day. When Daddy went to the farm to pick up his bride, Lester O'Dell, father of the bride, said to Daddy, "Now it's your turn to wait on that girl."

When our family would get ready to go somewhere together, Daddy started with the warnings at least fifteen minutes before we needed to depart. "Let's get this show on the road," he'd say. Then we'd sit in the car and wait, and Daddy would repeat in a quiet voice, "I wonder what she does in there?"

Daddy really appreciated all that Mom did every day. I think he was on a different time schedule. When she tried to do two days work in one, Daddy would say, "You've sure got it in overdrive today, haven't you, Honey?"

It seemed like Mom was always doing things for neighbors and friends. She hardly ever sat down. One day when she sat down for a minute, Elaine asked her if she had run out of work. After Mom laughed hysterically for a minute, she got up and flew into action again.

Mom had a gift of hospitality. She invited friends to dinner frequently and wanted no one to leave the table hungry. Our friends joined us sometimes for dinner, often with little notice. Mama said there was always enough. She took covered dishes to homes of shut-ins, elderly, and the bereaved. She gave her friends rides to appointments. She made homemade cottage cheese, butter, cakes, and pies which she gave away to friends or neighbors. She couldn't do enough for people. Her kindness didn't know how to quit.

Mom liked to watch a few television shows. *I Love Lucy* was definitely her favorite. However, she seldom sat down to watch the entire half hour show. She would combine her television watching with ironing, folding clothes, or sewing. *Art Linkletter's House Party* was one show that entertained her as she stood at the ironing board on Tuesdays.

There is an old Proverb that reads, "And in the evening, let not your hands stay idle." Cathy summed it up with this, "Grandma took that one and ran with it, didn't she?"

Mom belonged to many organizations and clubs. She hardly ever said "No" to any of their requests. She had a big heart, and she packed more into one day than anyone I've ever known.

After Elaine, Jim, and I were grown, we planned a wedding anniversary celebration for our folks. We had a goal. We hoped to keep Mom free of any work. We decided to hold the family dinner at the country club and let others do the preparations. We knew that it would be a challenge for Mom just to sit and be waited on, but we wanted to give it a try.

At the country club, Mom passed the butter dish several times and asked us if we wanted water refills or more rolls. She helped out with the baby in the highchair at the end of the table. It was Mom's nature to wait on people, to serve others. It was impossible to keep Mom sitting still for very long.

But on one count, we did succeed! It was a five minute car ride to the country club and a five minute ride back home. Mom sat down during both trips!

Mission accomplished!

The *BEDFORD Times Press*

The *Bedford Times Press* arrived today. It's like a letter from home, the closest thing to a visit with family.

About fifty years ago I graduated from Bedford High School. At the graduation ceremony our madrigal sang "Halls of Ivy." In that song, there's one line that captures my sentimental side. It is:

"As we sadly start our journeys far apart,

a part of every heart will linger here."

So that's it! A part of my heart lingers there, and when the *Times Press* arrives I feel connected again. Connected to places, people, and family who are still there.

There is a section of the paper called <u>Appreciation.</u> An out-of-towner wouldn't have to read very far to know that Bedford is filled with caring, unselfish, generous people. During illness, loss, and other hardships, it seems that friends and neighbors appear from every farm and house to help out. There are thank you notes for helping to celebrate a birthday by showing up with ice cream and a cake. How's that for making the newspaper?

The <u>Local News</u> elaborates on the almost daily events of a small segment of the population. These are the faithful residents, God love 'em, who report to Ellen about their latest activities. A former Bedfordite can make the <u>Local News</u> by going home and helping parents with household chores.

A stranger in town would immediately pick up on the celebration of longevity. Card showers for folks having birthdays of eighty and more are announced in advance, so the cards and letters can arrive on the big day. Then printed in the paper the following week might be a note of thanks from the recipients. That would appear in the <u>Appreciation</u> column, sometimes telling the exact number of cards that arrived in the mail.

Occasionally, a letter to the editor will enlighten the reader with opinions of the more out-spoken villagers, written and printed exactly the way it was verbalized.

State Representatives and Senators occasionally pay a visit and are sometimes photographed with a group of Bedfordites. The Reps and Senators are the ones who aren't wearing seed company or baseball caps.

It's important to notice the doctors' hours and days when they are assigned to Bedford. It's never a good idea to get sick on one of the days when the doctors visit other little towns.

The obituaries are listed in a column under the dark heading: <u>DEATHS.</u> I never miss reading these. The recently departed are frequently the parents of my friends, sad to say. Some of my contemporaries and classmates have been found in that column far too early.

<u>Birth</u> announcements, entitled <u>Wee Ones</u>, used to keep me posted on the offspring of my classmates. Now the new arrivals are the grandchildren and great grandchildren of my friends. Where *did* those years go?

The <u>Real Estate</u> ads are nothing short of unbelievable to this city dweller. Imagine the price of a house and several acres costing only $50,000! That might be a fraction of the down payment on a house in Southern California.

The <u>4H Club</u> reports tell of projects that have real importance to a child. How excited they must be when their names or pictures appear in the *Bedford Times Press.*

<u>Bulldogs</u> are the school mascots. All sports, both boys and lady bulldogs, are written up in almost as much detail as the Yankees in *The New York Times* or the Lakers

in *The Los Angeles Times*. Of course, the change in the school colors is a hot topic among discontented old-timers.

The small bergs around Bedford send their news to the *Times Press* office on a weekly basis. Usually weekly. Sometimes lack of newsworthy information or the weather prevents the trip into town. Gravity, Lenox, Hopkins, Blockton, Sharpsburg and New Market all have very small populations. Their close, long time friendships make up for lack of variety in big name entertainment and events. Getting together for a meal still seems to be the favorite form of Midwestern hospitality and entertainment.

The <u>For Rent</u> column tells of real bargains like a two bedroom home for a mere $350.00 a month.

<u>Hope O'Hara's</u> column is great for a chuckle and good reading. I appreciate her use of expanded vocabulary.

During the Taylor County Fair, there are several pages of photos of proud 4Hers with their prize animals. Those are amazing achievements, worthy of photos and awards. .

<u>Yard</u> and <u>Estate Sales</u> list antiques that could turn over a handsome profit if they were in an antique shop in a city.

Above the words *The Bedford Times Press* on the front page are the words: "Over 132 years of service to Bedford and Taylor County, Iowa." It used to say, "Printed Weekly and Read Daily." I like that sentiment!

A single copy of *The New York Times* costs 50 cents. A single copy of *The Bedford Times Press* costs me (an out-of-state subscriber) 63 cents. It may not equate, but it's worth every penny.

Billy Lambert
-Sanitation Engineer-

His shovel went into action
doing its work in the line up

Billy always wore a toothless smile,
scrubby bib overalls
and thermal underwear
when he followed
the horses down Main Street
in the annual Fourth of July parade.

Always a crowd pleaser
bystanders cheered him on
always asking the question,
"How's business, Billy?"

His reply was always the same.
"Pickin' up, pickin' up."

This true story was one that Uncle Ross loved to tell,
each time followed by his contagious laugh
and contented smile.

Chapter Nine

Siblings

My Brother, the Actor

It did not go unnoticed that most of my childhood memories include my sister, but not my little brother. Jim wasn't born until I was nine and a half years old. He grew up in a family that was different than Elaine's and mine, almost like an only child. One of the things that I remember about Jimmie is how his imagination worked overtime.

He was a one man football team, complete with a running commentary describing all the action on the field. He sat in the car or the bleachers with Mom and Dad watching the Friday night high school football games. Elaine and I were in the band or cheerleading by that time.

On Saturday mornings Jim was reenacting the game, all by himself. He became the star of the team in the uniform that he had created. Mom cut off a pair of old trousers. Jim donned a long sleeve knit shirt and padded up the shoulders. He wore his cardboard football helmet for protection! And with a football under one arm, he dashed across the back yard from Grandma's back door to ours, calling out the plays and the names of the players who were left behind on his way to a touchdown. He kept the announcer's excitement in his voice as he concluded, "And it's a TOUCHDOWN!" Then he'd recreate another play, acting out the parts of several of his favorite Bedford High School football heroes.

Recently Jim told me that he had several imaginary playmates. He didn't go into detail. That may not be the kind of thing a grown man talks about.

Jimmie loved rodeos. After seeing a rodeo, his imagination let him come exploding out of a shoot on a bucking bronco, sometimes using a stick horse, repeating the words of the announcer, "And now out of shoot number five is Brave Cowboy Jim on Dangerous Dy-no-mite!"

One of Jim's real life playmates was Denny Shepherd. They would go to a thrill show at the fair grounds and watch daredevils in automobiles flying across ramps. Back home they built bike ramps in the street and, with great bravery, rode their bicycles over the ramps, feeling the exhilaration of being airborne for a few seconds. I imagine Mom kept an eye on them.

Jim loved to pretend he was riding a horse in a race. His bicycle was his horse. He marked off starting points for the quarter mile race and the eighth mile race on Randolph Street. The finish line was in front of our house. Jim whipped his bicycle tire as he crossed the finish line. He imagined he was the winner of dozens of horse races. All this without leaving his yard or street! Just shows what a vivid and creative imagination will do for a kid!

Jim spent time with his animals and pets. His close friendship with his pet calf Buttercup is found in another chapter.

After Jim and Rosalyn moved back to Bedford and bought Grandpa Clyde's house, some changes were made. Keeping the living room, the front porch, and the second story rooms as they were, additions were made to the front and the back. What a great house it has become.

In more recent years, Bedford has been privileged to have several talented directors, and the town is full of actors and actresses. Several plays have thrilled the audiences at the High School Auditorium. Jim played many major roles. A list of his credits would put a famous Broadway actor to shame! Here are a few of them:

- Mortimer, the sane brother, "Arsenic and Old Lace" 1987
- Stage Manager, "Our Town" 1991
- Dr. Chumley, "Harvey" 1992
- Doc, "Those Crazy Ladies in the House on the Corner" 2003
- Aging Magazine Editor "You Can't Get There From Here."

The last play was performed in 2005 and to make it more fun, Jim's son Jeff had one of the leads. I would predict that Jeff also has a promising future in acting, because he makes it fun and does it so easily!

The town is fortunate to have the new Community Performing Arts Center at the high school.

Another venue for these talented performers has been the Historic Portrayals done on the Main Street of Bedford and in the local cemeteries. Central characters and founding fathers from the early days of Bedford come to life in the scripted portraits that have been accurately researched and well written by talented volunteer writers in town. The audience is divided into small groups, and they either walk or ride in a tram from one location to the next.

Bedford's Chamber/Main Street and the Taylor County Historical Society sponsored Living Cemetery Tours in 1999 and 2000.

Held at the old Bedford cemetery on May 16, 1999, Jim portrayed William W. Wilkins, a Civil War veteran who played the fife for Company F of the 9th Iowa Infantry. A typesetter by profession, he directed the Wilkins-Taylor County Band after the war. Jim still decorates the grave of Mr. Wilkins every Memorial Day. He felt a connection to his character.

Jeff portrayed a typical hobo who was buried in *Potters' Field*. It's a portion of the old Bedford cemetery with no gravestones. Jeff didn't waste an opportunity to ham it up, just a bit!

Our mother died that morning, on May 16, 1999. Jim and Jeff both felt that Mom would want them to perform as expected, so they did.

The following year the Living Cemetery Tour was held at Fairview Cemetery. Jeff portrayed Billy Lambert, early sanitation engineer. A poem entitled "Billy Lambert" appears elsewhere in this collection of stories. Uncle Ross liked to tell of personal encounters with Billy, who was a favorite character around town. Kind of makes you wonder how a humble outhouse cleaner could be so popular and well liked! Again, Jeff used his humor and charm to make this an unforgettable performance. Daddy was a part of the audience for this tour. At the end of Jeff's performance, his ad lib went something like this, "I'd like to shake hands with an old friend I haven't seen in years…Carl Cummings. How are ya? You might want to wash your hand now." Give Jeff a relaxed character to play, and he will relax it even more.

Jim portrayed John Van Fleet Crum, attorney and world record holder in the 220 yard dash. He was the world's fastest human at one time. He died at the age of 25, only three years after earning the honor. Jim puts a flower on the grave of John Van Fleet Crum every Memorial Day. It's the only flower there. Jim said that it just doesn't seem right that a former world's fastest human from Bedford, Iowa, should not be remembered. This shows the soft and sentimental side to my little brother. He has a good heart.

In 2001, the sponsors renamed the event, <u>Main Street Alive,</u> and the red brick streets of Main Street became the stage. Jim played Abram Clark Kinnison, who operated the Kinnison Livery Stable.

The next year, Jim was Harley Greenlee, a Civil War veteran who came to Bedford and built many of the brick buildings on Main Street. Getting into the role to a greater degree, Jim grew a beard for that part.

Bedford had a Sesquicentennial celebration in 2003. <u>Main Street Alive</u> performances added historical impact to the occasion. Jim portrayed the founder of Bedford, Edwin Houck. His great grandson was Paul Whiteman, the *King of Jazz*. Taking a break from a speaking part in 2004, Jim entertained the audience while singing bass in a barbershop quartet with John Standerford, David Dukes, and Dennis Crawford.

Jim got Rosalyn in the act the following year. In 2005 they portrayed A.C. and Phoebe Brice. A.C. Brice, a politician, was named Consul General to Cuba. Phoebe was a tireless worker in the Presbyterian Church in Bedford. She organized the weeklong revival meetings when Billy Sunday came to Bedford in 1900. Imagine! Billy Sunday in Bedford!

Coming full circle, Jim played the part of Isaac W. Scherich in 2006.

Jim wrote the script for this performance. Mr. Scherich was the builder of our house at 608 Randolph Street. There is more on I. W. Scherich in the first chapter.

The most recent performance of Main Street Alive, 2007, followed a different format. A stage was erected in the court yard. Performers were famous people in the country as well as early Bedford founders. Jim was William Jennings Bryan, the keynote speaker of Bedford's first ever Chautauqua in 1904. Ten thousand people in Bedford heard William Jennings Bryan speak that day in 1904 *without a microphone*. Jim's research included a tidbit about Bryan: when he spoke the tent poles shook!

Dad portrayed William Jennings Bryan at Bedford's Centennial Pageant in 1953. Like father, like son.

There are several ways to share a history lesson. Main Street Alive and Living Cemetery Tours are more creative and a lot more fun than textbooks. I suspect that Jim's vivid imagination as a little kid has been an asset in his acting career!

When the Methodist Church in Bedford observed its sesquicentennial in November of 2004, my brother reenacted the role of his great, great grandfather, Rev. Jesse Herbert. This ancestor was a charter member of the Bedford Methodist Church. Jim's script is found in Appendix 5.

Jim wrote it, memorized it, and performed it. I'm quite proud of my little brother, the actor, the veterinarian, and the youngest in our family. It is quite possible that he was the favorite child!

My Sister, the Middle Child

No one ever asks us where we want to be in the family line-up. We are born into a family and fit in according to our birth order.

I don't remember being the only child, although I was the only child for two years and two months. Elaine and I grew up much like twins, experiencing a lot of *firsts* together.

When little brother Jimmie was born, Elaine had to relinquish her place as the youngest and make room for the new baby. She became the middle child.

If there was one sentence that Mom must have said a million times, it was, "Learn to share." Elaine and I shared *everything:* clothes, toys, a double bed, a bedroom, ideas, a bicycle, household chores, germs, pets, measles, mumps, and chicken pox, laughter, heartaches, and serious girl talks. We shared similar interests and talents. We played piano and cornet duets. We sang vocal duets. I think we even shared a boy friend once, although briefly.

Being away from home during my first year at college put a kink in our wardrobes. Borrowing a favorite sweater or necklace wasn't as easy anymore. More than her clothes, I missed Elaine. She seemed like my other half, the kid sister who was always there doing everything with me most of the time. Thankfully, we are still close in heart.

Elaine's talent as a comedian began to sprout somewhere in elementary school. It came in handy when I was about to get blamed for something that we did wrong. It's not easy being the oldest.

Little sister's bubbly personality brought her a <u>Miss Congeniality</u> title in the *Miss Iowa Beauty Pageant* in the 1950s. I admire and respect her and consider myself lucky to be her sister.

My brother, sister, and I all got married at the age of twenty-two. We all had our daughters first and our sons second. Jim and I have one daughter and one son. Elaine doubled our numbers. We gave our parents an even number of granddaughters and grandsons, four of each. From oldest to youngest, they are Cathy, Steve, Peg, Susan, Matt, Carla, Ben, and Jeff.

Elaine and I both became teachers, following in Mom's footsteps. By the time we became teachers, it was acceptable for the woman to work outside of the home—a different climate than our mother's era. Actually, at that time there were three acceptable jobs/careers for young women after college graduation. Those three were teaching, nursing, and secretarial/office work.

Elaine chose music as her major and taught in many public schools in Iowa. Musical performances, programs, and concerts have delighted audiences of parents and grandparents throughout the state, thanks to her ability to organize, teach, and create enthusiasm and memories for kids. Being married to a Methodist pastor, Elaine has been Dick's secretary, co-pastor, driver, organist, music director, spiritual partner, inspiration, and encourager.

Every time she emails me a poem (she calls them pomes), I'm reminded of how easily she can make me laugh.

Elaine believes that her greatest contribution to the world is not her musical talents, not her pomes or sense of humor, but her years as a mother and a wife.

Elaine and Dick are grandparents of three granddaughters and three grandsons. They may drive for hours to see one of their grandchildren in a sporting event or musical program. They are doing what they love to do.

Elaine is my daughter's middle name. She's named after her Aunt Elaine, the innocent, funny, amazing, and talented middle child…my little sister.

CHAPTER TEN

Cherished Memories

Sunday Evening Telephone Chats

Alexander Graham Bell's invention, developed only one year after the house at 608 Randolph Street was built, has kept families connected for over 130 years.

His invention has kept me in touch with my Iowa family since 1960, during the years when I lived in Colorado, Minnesota, and California.

When their grandchildren were small, Mom and Daddy usually initiated the telephone calls. That was during the 60s and 70s. After that things began to change.

I called about half of the time, and Mom did most of the talking. She asked about Cathy and Steve. Then she told me what she was doing, always busy with sewing, knitting, quilting, canning, or getting ready for club or a church activity.

I'd ask the question, "Daddy, are you on the extension?"

He'd reply, "Yes, Honey, I'm just listening."

When the conversation began to wind down, Daddy would conclude with his line, "Well, I believe you girls have just about covered all the news." Before he hung up, he might remind me that Mother had a difficult time "closing" a conversation.

Then, years later, during our telephone visits, it seemed that Mom had a difficult time finishing her thoughts. She couldn't remember names of people. Daddy would finish her sentences for her. He seemed to know exactly what she wanted to say.

I initiated the weekly Sunday night telephone calls most of the time after that.

One evening I had a specific question for Mom. "How do you make your famous apple butter, Mom?"

Mom said she couldn't quite remember but would look for the recipe. She looked in the kitchen, opening cupboards and drawers while Daddy and I continued to talk. Finally, Mom said she couldn't seem to find her recipe. Daddy knew the procedure for making apple butter, and he tactfully coached Mom through the steps, so she got the credit and I got the recipe.

Realizing that my parents' relationship was going through some major changes, I never wanted to miss calling them on a Sunday night, sometimes more often.

We all began to realize that Mom's symptoms of dementia were getting worse. Daddy continued to be Mom's caregiver for the next several years. This, he believed, was his responsibility to the marriage and to her. In the two years between 1996 and 1998, Dad had four heart attacks. I talked to him from his hospital room on each of those occasions and sometimes took a flight back home to Iowa.

Jim and Rosalyn had the major responsibility for Mom and Dad, God love them. It's the most difficult job in the world, but a job that you never want to end.

Daddy had triple by-pass heart surgery in February of 1998. We spoke frequently on the phone. I told him I'd be there when he went back home.

Mom was unable to stay alone while Daddy was in the hospital. While she waited for Daddy to return, she stayed at the Bedford Nursing and Rehab Center. When it became apparent that her condition needed to be evaluated, she went to an Omaha hospital. The diagnosis made there was one that we already expected. She had Alzheimer's with depression.

While Mom was going through the evaluation in Omaha, Daddy came home from the hospital. With tears in his eyes, he told me that that was the first time he returned home and Mom wasn't there waiting for him. Sadly, she was never able to return home.

Later, Mom went to a convalescent facility in Missouri Valley, Iowa, where she could get the proper care. She was near Elaine and Dick who became her closest family caregivers. Carla lived there, also, and went to see her Grandma frequently. I missed the Sunday night telephone conversations with my mother. It was through my telephone connections with Elaine that I was informed about Mom's activities and health issues.

After February 1998, the weekly telephone calls to Daddy became more important than ever, as he continued to live alone at 608 Randolph. Our Sunday evening telephone chats became a cherished part of my week. Sometimes Elaine would call him before I did, then he could update me with the happenings of my siblings and their families.

"Hi, Daddy. How's everything?" I'd ask.

"Well, hello, Honey. I'm fine. How's everything in California?" His response always seemed so upbeat and positive.

He seemed really happy to get my calls. Sometimes we'd talk for an hour. The weekend came up with a huge missing part if I didn't hear Daddy's voice. It was during those Sunday night telephone conversations over the next five years that I learned much more about my Dad's life and his views on the world. We connected in a deeper, more sensitive way.

Our last telephone conversations were more difficult. During his last few months, Daddy stayed at the Bedford Nursing and Rehab Center in Bedford, with Hospice care being provided. About two weeks before Daddy passed away, Jim took his cell phone to Daddy's room. It was a Sunday night. Jim called me and handed the phone to Daddy.

He had difficulty hearing and speaking while on oxygen, so we made our conversation a brief one. I would always close our telephone conversations with "I love you," and Daddy would repeat the same words to me. I believe that the last words that I heard my Dad say were, "I love you." What a fine memory. What a grand legacy!

The first Father's Day without Daddy was only a couple of weeks after his death. I was home in California by that time. My friends knew that it wasn't an easy time for me. Many of them shared with me on that day that they had never had much of a relationship with their own dads, and Father's Day didn't hold much meaning for them. It hurts me to realize what they missed.

For people who haven't been honored with parents who lived to be 90 something with reasonably good health, I feel sad for them. Elaine and Jim and I have been blessed with parents who celebrated many wedding anniversaries. That's a lot of memories, good times, a wide range of emotions, and "lots of love," the phrase that Mom used to sign her letters. The few letters that I have saved are as valuable as rare museum treasures. Now I understand why people save old letters. The "writing" speaks to us long after the voice has been silenced.

Sunday evenings still seem like the perfect time to pick up the phone and call family. Sometimes I can still hear my parents' voices…a long way off in a memory. Almost like our treasured weekly Sunday evening telephone chats.

A Spark Rekindled

Alzheimer's is a cruel disease. One moment things can seem fairly normal, the next, far from it.

Daddy didn't make too many attempts to visit Mom after she moved to the Alzheimer's unit in Missouri Valley, Iowa. It was far too painful for him.

A family dinner was planned for the occasion of Mom's 93rd birthday. The day was April 30, 1999. I was in Iowa at the time. I drove Daddy to Elaine and Dick's home in Missouri Valley, Iowa. Jim and Rosalyn took the time off from work to be there too. Elaine prepared a wonderful dinner complete with a birthday cake. It was a time for Mom and Daddy to be together with their three children and spouses.

While Elaine and I went to the Nursing Home to pick up Mom, Daddy decided to wait for us at Elaine's house. Mom seemed confused and wondered where we were going. It took both of us to assist her in getting in and out of the car. We helped her into the house where Daddy was waiting.

As we entered the living room, Mom saw Daddy and for the sweetest moment had a look of pleasant surprise on her face. She recognized him! Daddy's serious expression changed into a big smile, just for Mom. She brightened up; her step quickened. They met, touched, and kissed each other with their usual conservative display of affection. Mom's words of surprise were, "Well, there you are!"

If God could have given a sweeter gift on the occasion of Mom's last birthday on earth, I don't know what it could have been. As Elaine and I fought back the tears, we all knew that for a brief moment, a spark had been rekindled. It's a moment that remains crystal clear for me, and I am so grateful that it does. I know that Daddy treasured that poignant moment for the rest of his life. I believe we all knew that that day would be the last time all of us would be together on earth.

When it came time for me to catch a plane back to California, I hugged everyone "good-bye." Daddy gave me a big hug along with a special blessing by being the first one to say, "I love you."

Keeping my composure is a challenge when it's time to say the "good-byes." Climbing into my rental car for the drive to the Omaha airport, I waved one more time and managed to keep myself together all the way to the end of the alley.

Two weeks later, our Lord invited Mom to her heavenly home and to another kind of celebration. I'm absolutely sure that Jesus plans a loving "welcome home" party for His own--a party that's simply out of this world!

Found

The box was found. I never realized that it was lost. In fact, I didn't know it existed. Each time I went back home to Iowa, Mom reminded me of some things in my upstairs bedroom closet. I honestly thought that I had completely vacated that old north bedroom closet, but Mom kept telling me that there was an unfinished task waiting for me.

While cleaning out the house that had been Mom and Daddy's home for sixty-nine years, Elaine found the box. It was sitting on the floor, buried in the back of the closet. Even as Elaine carried the heavy box out of the room and placed it before me, I still couldn't imagine what it contained.

Opening the flaps on the battered box was like opening shutters on a window to my past. The event was made better because it was shared with Elaine and a high school friend, Phyllis Jones.

Lying in the box were many scrapbooks. The most recent mementoes were on the top, the books of the earliest years on the bottom, neatly and chronologically stacked in the box. I began to have a vague memory of them.

The scrapbooks from college years (1957-1960) were on top. I looked at programs and newspaper clippings from plays, musicals, and style shows. Black and white photos of friends on campus and in the dorm filled a photo album. My report cards, a Baccalaureate Program, and graduation programs were found along with a copy of my diploma: Bachelor of Science in Secondary Education. I wondered where that was. Those years seem like a life time ago!

The scrapbooks of high school years had even more *keepers*. I found programs of band concerts, piano recitals, junior and senior play scripts and programs, musicals, Rainbow stuff, dance books and corsages from proms, graduation programs, even report cards of almost every subject for each year of high school. So many reminders of my busy teenage high school years. Did I really save all of these? Phyllis couldn't believe it. Neither could I.

Elaine summed it up perfectly when she concluded, "We were taught to save." Did I organize these things into tidy scrapbooks and photo albums? When did I have time to do that? Perhaps Mom did it; that might explain why she continued to remind me of my unfinished business.

It was entirely unthinkable for Mom to throw away anything without asking first. Bless her heart. I missed her and wished she could have shared the experience with me as I went through a lifetime of treasures.

We uncovered things that brought back memories: an imprinted napkin of a cousin's wedding, a Mother-Daughter banquet program, church bulletins, and countless other reminders.

We were amused at some of the things. I even saved a nut cup from a wedding shower. Imagine! It was a melancholy journey.

There was a scrapbook for each school year. My grade cards were inside each book, from kindergarten to my senior year. Miss Alice Hale's signature was on my kindergarten report card. It was dated 1944-45. My first grade teacher was Mrs. Bailey. I remembered her signature in that beautiful cursive handwriting that so many of our teachers had.

I had two second grade teachers, Mrs. Krug and Mrs. Davison. My third grade teacher was Miss Johnston. Miss Dory taught fourth grade. There were grade cards from Miss Polton, my fifth grade teacher, and Mrs. Donovan for sixth grade. Completing the collection were report cards for most of the junior high and high school subjects. Unbelievable!

Having lived in thirteen apartments, houses, or condos since leaving 608 Randolph Street in 1960, I've had to be very selective with my *keepers*.

All of the things that I decided to save, mostly report cards and photographs, fit into a large brown envelope. I packed it in the bottom of the cedar chest, a gift to Mom from Daddy in 1934, the year in which they were married. The cedar chest and a few other special pieces of furniture were placed on a moving van and transported to California for my kids and me. That was in July of 2003.

I have learned this: treasures in cedar chests, cupboards, closets, and attics have surprise value for generations to come. I must remember to tuck away a few surprises in my closets and cupboards for my kids to find someday! I hope they remember to look for the brown envelope at the bottom of the cedar chest!

I'm Home

There's my brother waiting for me at his front door.
It's midnight and I'm driving into his driveway at last.
After the 100 mile drive in the rain, in a rental car,
and six hours of airports and airplanes before that,
I finally let myself listen to my weary body.
It feels like every muscle aches.

But for now,
there's a warm hug,
someone to help me with a suitcase
that I've wrestled with all day,
a cozy kitchen with two cups of warm drink
sitting on the kitchen table.
The relief is beyond description.
What pleasure to be with family,
to be in the house
that sits next to my childhood home…
the dark and empty house, next door at 608 Randolph.

Was it only 36 hours ago
that Jim called to tell me
that Dad was worse and back in the hospital?
Knowing that the next two weeks

would be spent with Dad in a hospital room
was never easy,
but I wanted to be there.
Uncertain March weather in Iowa
can make the twenty-two mile trip to the hospital
unpredictable, at best.

But that's tomorrow
and the next day
and the day after that.
But for now, the long trip is over
and a warm bed is waiting for me upstairs.
I'm home.

Saying Goodbye

During my parents last days and months, it was a tremendous comfort to know that Elaine and Dick and Jim and Rosalyn were never far away from Mom and Daddy. I appreciated them more than any words can ever express. They kept me informed by telephone, and whenever possible, I flew home to Bedford. There are times when being almost two thousand miles from family can be a real disadvantage. I began to associate airports with saying "goodbye."

Alzheimer's disease made my mother's goodbye a slow one. We saw the gradual decline happen over a period of several years. One thing that never changed was her gentle, sweet disposition. She was called the "little sweetie" at the nursing home in Missouri Valley, Iowa, her last address on earth. We are grateful for that.

After our family reunion on Mom's 93rd birthday, her decline was rapid. Sixteen days later, she entered the presence of our Lord early on the morning of May 16, 1999. I was expecting the phone call in the pre-dawn hours.

I spoke with Jim and Elaine and Daddy several times that day. The stories that they shared were assurances of God's presence and protection. In Missouri Valley, Iowa, Elaine gathered up Mom's things and made several trips from the nursing home to her car. Each time, she was greeted by a bright red cardinal making his appearance near the door. A mourning dove, in the distance, gave an echo. Mom had always loved birds, knew their various calls, their nesting habits, and names. Her favorite color was red.

Jim, also, noticed that the mourning doves were in full chorus that morning as he approached Dad's house to give him the news about Mom.

With airline reservations made for the following morning and a suitcase packed, I prepared to take my daily walk. I was feeling a long way from Iowa. I hoped God would give me a sign of His presence to help me feel close to family and close to nature.

I had never seen nor heard doves along my usual walking path. But that day was different. I could hardly believe my eyes and ears. From roof tops, in trees, and on the telephone lines, mourning doves serenaded me. I stopped. Still unbelieving, I listened to their gentle, soothing voices and said a quiet "Thank you." I no longer felt alone.

The casket spray of red and white carnations and roses delivered to the funeral home contained two red cardinals. Pastor Ruth gave a memorable service. At the cemetery the last two verses of Jude and the twenty-third Psalm left us with a sense of peace. Mom was laid to rest beside her infant son.

Elaine and Dick, Jim and Rosalyn, Daddy and I wrote hundreds of thank you acknowledgements in the next few days. It seemed good to be with family in a small community. Each day following Mom's service, Elaine and I walked to the cemetery in keeping with our daily walking routines. We noticed a bright red cardinal playfully darting from tree to tree along the walking route. She accompanied us every day, looking like a young bird who was trying out her wings for the first time. Perhaps she was on a mission to remind us of our mother's protective presence, her new life free of disease, and God's peace.

I stayed in Iowa with Daddy for a couple of weeks. The spring weather seemed perfect. The time to leave came too soon, and the "good bye" was harder than ever.

Jim and Rosalyn became the main caregivers for Daddy. Our Sunday evening telephone chats were special times for me. Being a retired person, I was able to make more frequent trips to Iowa over the next four years. During those years Daddy stayed in his home, determinedly riding his exercise bicycle five miles each day and expressing gratitude to Jim and Rosalyn for their daily visits and help. I never heard my Dad say a negative word or unkind remark about anyone.

During the winter of 2000, Daddy was gravely ill. He had pneumonia and was hospitalized for several weeks. In a vision or a dream, he came to the River Jordan, perhaps a brief glimpse of the other side. The loving presence of our Lord began to show him the way over an elusive bridge to the other side. He saw Mama and other family members waving and encouraging him to cross the bridge. But it was revealed to him that it wasn't yet his time to cross over to the other side. There was one more assignment for Daddy to complete on earth. He felt a heavy sadness as he returned to his earthly body. His recovery was slow. He never knew exactly what his last assignment was, but we knew that God would work out the details. There was someone, somewhere on earth, who needed to spend some time with my Dad, to listen to his wisdom, lighten up with his wit, and learn about his faith in God.

One time he told me that if given the chance to live his life over again, he wouldn't change a thing.

I was in Bedford for Christmas 2002. In Dr. Kopp's office with Jim and me, Daddy agreed to go to the nursing home for the winter. It may have been the hardest thing he ever had to do. He told me that he wanted his kids to know he was safe and eating well, and that having people around might be just fine. After he got settled in his chair in his room, he told me that he didn't believe he would ever be going back to Randolph Street again. He accepted this change in his life so bravely. He did it for his children. He set an incredible example for all of us.

The hospital in Corning, Iowa, and the Bedford Nursing and Rehab. Center became the final addresses for Daddy as he battled illnesses for the next several months. I returned again in March. Spending two weeks visiting with Dad in the Corning Hospital was an opportunity for us to share stories as I took copious notes. Jim and Elaine kept me informed by telephone after I returned to California.

On May 31, 2003, my telephone rang at 4:22 A.M. I had not slept. I knew Jim would be calling. Daddy died on his oldest grandchild's birthday. He received his transfer just short of his 96th birthday-- his last assignment completed.

Another flight to Kansas City, the usual rental car routine, and a drive north to Iowa, one that I had made only two months earlier. I stayed alone in the empty house at 608 Randolph Street.

It was good to be with family, my sister and brother, cousins, nieces, nephews, and Auntie Blanche. Preparations were made for Dad's service. An expression of sympathy in small communities is shown by bringing food to the family. Rosalyn became an expert manager of the food in her kitchen. No one was ever hungry with the generous donations brought in by many friends.

Three pastors shared in Daddy's service. One of them was Jim's childhood friend, Dennis Shepherd. Daddy was laid to rest in the family plot beside Mom and baby Richard, near his parents Clyde and Florence, and his brother-in-law, Dale.

For the next several weeks, Elaine and Jim and I began the overwhelming task of sorting through our parents' lifetime accumulation of belongings and saying "good bye" to much of it.

My parents' youngest grandson, Jeff and his wife Tara became the new owners of *608 Randolph Street* in August of 2003. It seems so right for the house to stay in our family.

For a melancholy like me, it would be extremely difficult to say "good bye" to the old house, too.

Appendix 1

The Enid, Oklahoma, newspaper article:

ENID SOLDIER RELATES DAYS WITH LINCOLN

I.W. Scherich, 823 West Randolph,
Saw Famous President Five Times

SPEAKS KINDLY OF WORDS OF LEADER

"Emancipator" Honored On
Each Side of
Mason-Dixon Line

There is one citizen of Enid (PA.) to whom the coming of Lincoln's birthday is more than a national affair. While serving in the army of the Potomac, he stood beside the carriage wheel of the great war-time president and watched the light of the afternoon sun play over the kindly face of the man who was soon to become a nation's martyr.

I. W. Scherich, 823 West Randolph, enlisted in Company "A" of the Eighteenth Pennsylvania Cavalry early in 1862 and was assigned to the defense of Washington. Many are the stories he can tell of the visits of Lincoln to the army camps and how it was the president's habit to leave his carriage and walk among the soldiers.

The first time Mr. Scherich saw Lincoln was in January 1863.

His regiment was marched in review up Pennsylvania Avenue while Lincoln stood at the front steps of the White House. Less than a week later the president visited their camp near Arlington—in fact, two visits to the camp were made while Mr. Scherich was there.

WAS AT GETTYSBURG

Then from the defenses of Washington, the Eighteenth Pennsylvania was hurled into the Gettysburg campaign. Under General Farnsworth they came upon the field the second day and went immediately into action.

The story of those four July days has been told over and over in history and song. Farnsworth died and with him, in his brilliant charge against the Confederate lines, died many of the men of the Eighteenth.

Lee's invasion of the north failed and the theater of war shifted to the fields of Virginia.

Scherich's company was restored to war strength and under leader after leader went through the many heartbreaking campaigns along the Richmond-Washington Road. At last in August 1864, worn and tattered from the incessant fighting in the Wilderness and around Petersburg, the regiment went into camp at Stoneman not far down the Potomac from Washington.

For a week it had rained incessantly; the spirits of the men were drooping. The hardest kind of fighting had been theirs. Under Colonel Dalgreen they had even penetrated the

Confederate lines around Richmond in an attempt to release the prisoners of Belle Isle and the infamous pens of Libby. This, they might have done had not a black man led them astray in an attempt to ford the North Ann. Dalgreen was killed but not until he had ordered the faithless black man shot.

REGIMENT NEARLY ANNIHILATED

The regiment was nearly annihilated but fought its way northward. At Beaver's Dam, Lee's supplies were destroyed and with a Virginia ham at each cavalryman's saddle they made their way through the Wilderness to Mechanicsville, where in a night camp, Confederate artillery shelled the weakened forces and drove them northward.

We were a sorry looking but seasoned regiment of horsemen that began making camp at Stoneman. Before the camp was completed, a picket called, "The president is coming." With cheers the men left their work and ran to the road. Lincoln drove through the camp but did not stop. The cheering soldiers watched him from sight and then returned to pitching the tents.

But Lincoln was a man that did not forget and he had a warm place in his heart for the men who bore the brunt of the fighting. He sent them word that he would return, and true to his promise, four days later, the men drew up in formation to receive the commander-in-chief with military honors.

Lincoln's cortege came into the camp and the president asked his coachman to stop. He could not pass by the men with the grime and carnage of the Wilderness still upon their uniforms. With him were three high officers that Mr. Scherich did not know. They remained seated but Lincoln, with his six feet four stature, stood erect in the carriage and greeted the cheering soldiers.

"In his tall hat," said Mr. Scherich, "he looked taller than he really was. He was dressed in a Prince Albert coat, while his trousers seemed twice as large as necessary for his long legs. A full minute he looked at us, his face serious; his eyes seeming to take in every detail of our appearance. Then he began to speak.

"You have just come from the Wilderness. You have given a good account of yourselves there. I congratulate you on your bravery and steadfastness." For three minutes or more he talked to us. His language was simple; his words were those of a soldier talking to soldiers. He spoke of our hardships and of what was being done to bring the war to a close. Only his opening and closing words am I able to remember after these sixty-two years.

Then, over the face of the president seemed to pass a shadow. "Your work is not done. You are going into the valley (Shenandoah) under Sheridan. You will have hard fighting there, I expect, but hope it will soon be over. I hope this thing won't last much longer."

Lincoln then sat down, nodded to his coachman and was driven rapidly away. I never saw him again but true to his promise we went into the Shenandoah with Sheridan and true to his prediction we found hard fighting there. At Winchester, I left my arm, shot off charging the rebel lines. Comrades led my horse behind a hill and there I found my mess-mate of many campaigns, shot through the breast, dead.

"It was in September, 1864, that I was wounded and after many weeks in a Philadelphia hospital, I arrived at my rural home, back in the Pennsylvania hills. The war was over; everyone was rejoicing. There were no daily newspapers in rural communities then, so news traveled slowly. But the ninth of April, 1865, had come and word trickled in to us that Lee had surrendered at Appomattox. The war was indeed over!"

REJOICING SHORT LIVED

But our rejoicing was short lived. On the fifteenth of April, like wildfire across the country by word of mouth, came the news that Lincoln had been assassinated. The nation stood stunned, but I doubt if any felt as great sorrow as the soldiers he had commanded. And sorrow was felt in the South as well as in the North. I am not sure but what the South recognized the greatness of Lincoln even before we of the North did.

"The years have passed," concluded Mr. Scherich, "but I have never forgotten how Lincoln looked. There are few pictures that really do him justice. There was something in the face of Lincoln, something in his long, awkward frame, that the cameras have failed to catch.

I never saw him smile, but even in his seriousness there seemed to be homely tolerance and kindly humor that won everyone with whom he came in contact."

Appendix 2

Among the findings in the house at 608 Randolph Street was an account of some of the events in the life of my father's grandfather, **Alonzo Cummings**. As a member of the **National Society of the Daughters of the American Revolution**, I believe it is a privileged duty to preserve family records and stories. It is through this line of descendents that the females in the Cummings family are eligible to join the Daughters of the American Revolution.

Typed on four pages of onion skin paper, the print had become extremely faded. Perhaps these pages were typed by my father, who as a young boy loved to sit with his grandfather in their rocking chairs on the porch.

Alonzo, who became blind in his old age, loved to spend time with his grandson, Carl, telling him stories of his childhood and his years of fighting during the Civil War.

These pages contain some of those stories.

Alonzo Cummings

Here are the memories of Alonzo Cummings, known as Lonnie, in his boyhood days; he was the same lad who came to Appanoose County, Iowa, in the year of 1854 with his father and two younger brothers and a sister, who was the youngest in the family.

His father, George, settled on a farm south of Moravia (southeastern Iowa), after coming from Perry County, Indiana, in 1854. Lonnie's mother had passed away perhaps one or two years prior to George's decision of coming to Iowa. His younger brother, Eli, and a sister,

Elizabeth, who was married to either Conrad or Elijah Link, perhaps helped with her brother George's family.

They had three or four wagons and four teams and one yoke of cattle belonging to George. They crossed the Illinois prairie. Coming to the Mississippi River, they crossed on a boat powered by oars. A wagon and a team were all that it would accommodate at one time. They also brought four or five cows, and a heifer or two. In crossing the river, a heifer jumped the railing. Since Eli was a good swimmer, he swam out and threw a rope around her horns and towed her on across behind the boat.

In 1855 Alonzo, being the oldest child, helped his father, George, on the new land, putting in the crops and in a few years was plowing. His father used the horse team and Alonzo used the yoke of cattle. Alonzo could turn the yoke of cattle at the corners of the field before his father could turn this team of horses.

Alonzo, while in his early teens, and possibly some other boys, walked from Moravia, Iowa, to a place called Orleans in eastern Appanoose County where there was a public hanging of a man accused of poisoning his wife. The man's name was Hinkle.

Alonzo, or Lonnie, was growing pretty fast by January of 186l. The war clouds were looking dark between the states. In April of 1861 war was declared against the South. Lincoln, acting on the Congress of the United States, called for 75,000 volunteers. This was soon filled and a second call for 125,000 was made. These men were to serve three years or longer if the war lasted longer.

Alonzo, not being 18 until January 1862, had difficulty volunteering. He was large enough, weighing 175 pounds in his stocking feet, as that was the way they were accepted. But he wasn't old enough for this Iowa Regiment without his father's consent. His father signed for him but by this time the Regiment was completed and he could not be accepted.

In late September, David Moore of Canton, Missouri, volunteered to raise the First Northeast Missouri Infantry. Alonzo and eleven other men enlisted and he was the first to be called to duty. Here are the words of Colonel Moore, which he posted in northeast Missouri and southern Iowa.

"All who are willing to fight for their homes and their loved ones and the glorious flag of the Union are invited to join. Bring guns and ammunition until the government can aid us. We must take care of ourselves. Secessionists and rebel traitors desiring a fight can be accorded on demand."

Humphrey W. Woodard, in 1861, was authorized to raise the Second Missouri Infantry but both men failed to raise the regiments and they consolidated the 1st and 2nd. D. Moore appointed Colonel Woodard Lieutenant Colonel, and the Regiment was called the 21st Missouri. It was the first one raised. After the Regiment was sworn in, there were acts of disloyal persons, which resulted in an engagement in the little towns or villages of Craton and Athens. Not too long ago, these still showed the works of violence.

After this the Regiment was sent to Jefferson Barracks, Missouri, getting ready for what was to come later.

While a young soldier, Cummings was still at Jefferson Barracks. General Sterling Price of Kentucky, started north to raid northern Missouri.

The 21st Missouri was ordered with other Regiments and the 3rd Iowa Cavalry to go in pursuit of Price. He had raided portions of Missouri burning their homes and killing people. This was in February and March of 1862. They had no place to go. This soldier remembers the muddy roads and spring rains that made this march so hard to forget.

The Colonel of the Regiment, D. Moore, as well as other regiments and cavalry, tried to head off Price. But Price changed his course and went to Arkansas. We followed

Price as far west as Independence, Missouri. There we were ordered back to Jefferson Barracks, but not for long. We were issued new clothing, which was badly needed by April 1st. We then went to St. Louis and rode a steamer on the Mississippi River to the mouth of the Tennessee River, and we landed at Pittsburg Landing, Tennessee.

We were assigned to the 6th Division commanded by General Prentiss. Alonzo was appointed Corporal and on Sunday night it was his time to post the guard. They were on duty for two hours and off for four hours.

About 4 A.M. on a Monday morning, April 6th, he had posted the last relief and went back to where some other soldiers had a fire, for it was chilly on early April mornings, even in Tennessee. "I had not been there but a few minutes," said Corporal Cummings, "until we heard firing in the distance. It kept getting closer as the minutes went by." They told each other, "We are being attacked. The Confederates are driving the pickets in."

We began falling back toward our quarters. Before we got there the regiment was forming, bugles were sounding and companies were forming. Colonel Moore was giving orders to companies, but some were out of ammunition so he gave the orders to fit bayonets and charge. He had only gone a short distance when I noticed a group of orderlies were removing the Colonel's horse that had been shot. The Colonel had lost a leg. Meanwhile, Regiments were going to the right and left, so the Lieutenant Colonel took command and ordered us to move.

After Shiloh we went into Kentucky to Paducah. It was September 1862 and we went to Tuka to meet Van dorn's Confederate Army.

About the time we got Van dorn out of Tuka, there was Tupilo, where there was some hard fighting with Forrest's Cavalry, only a short time before we defeated and captured some of the 3rd Iowa Cavalry at Guntown,

Mississippi. Among them was Benjamin Fulk who was taken to Andersonville, a Confederate prison in Georgia. Grant sent A. J. Smith and the 21st Missouri Infantry and some Iowa Cavalry to Tupilo, Mississippi, to fight General Forrest. He was severely beaten and they retreated.

In October, 1862, the Regiment had advanced to Carinth, Mississippi. The hot sun shone down on us as we lay there in the battle line. The Confederate cannons were throwing shells among us. One cannon struck a few yards from our front line. It failed to explode, but then continued bouncing and struck two soldiers. One was Anderson York of Bloomfield, Iowa. He was unfit for duty for some time. The other soldier regained his breath and let loose a few words of profanity before he was taken to the hospital. The Captain bawled out the other Sergeant, who was hurt. The shell lay there and sizzled until it cooled. It was then taken to Ordinance Depot.

After two hours we were ordered forward to support a battery. We lay under the cannon in front of the wheels and were given orders for no one to fire until orders were given to the gunners. I lay there wondering if our officers were going to let the Confederates take us without firing a shot. The enemy was forming three lines deep to take the battery at bayonet point, but when they got to within fifty or sixty yards of us, the orders came to fire. Muskets let loose like hundreds of firecrackers. The battery let loose a murderous fire and in a short time the smoke was so thick you could see only a short distance. Orders came to cease fire. The Confederates had fallen back but were forming again. Soon they were coming again, but could get no closer than the first time. Orders were given to cease firing.

I could have walked twenty-five steps and never stepped on the ground for dead Confederate soldiers. The officers said it was too bad to have to kill so many brave men, but that is war.

In December, 1864, General Hood, the Confederate Commander of southern forces, replaced General Johnson.

General Grant and the War Department in Washington ordered Thomas, who commanded the 16th Army Corps, to which I belonged, to proceed to Nashville to capture or destroy Hood's army. General Thomas attacked on the 14th of December, and defeated Hood on the 15th and 16th so effectively that Hood's army was never unified again.

History of Cummings family

Isaiah Cummings. Mexican War 1846

George Cummings (father of Alonzo) Union Army, Civil War. 36th Iowa Infantry. Died of fever in Memphis, Tennessee. Buried in Memphis.

Eli Cummings. 36th Iowa Infantry, Wounded at Marks Mill, Arkansas, on April 25, 1864. Died as a result of the wounds at Little Rock, Arkansas.

William H. Cummings, Union Army, Civil War, Kentucky Cavalry

Titus Cummings, Union Army, Civil War, Company G 81st Indiana Infantry, Wounded at Battle of Chickamauga, September 9, 1864.

Appendix 3

The Rose Bush

In 1843 George Cummings bought a rose bush for his bride. The English rose was a delicate pink color; the heart-shaped petals made it unique. She treasured it, cared for it, and kept it protected from the harsh Indiana winters. Part of their land washed down the Ohio River during the heavy spring rains. With determination the young couple farmed their land, a gift from his father, and survived the dangerously exciting prairie life. The year following their marriage, they were blessed with a son.

George and Frances were successful at adding to their farmland and also to their family. In the next seven years of their marriage she bore him two more sons and a baby daughter. And then she died.

The grief-stricken young widower placed roses from her rose bush on her grave. George's older sister Elizabeth stayed with the young family for a season, tending to the children, the garden, and nurturing the rose bush.

The following year, George had made up his mind. He wanted to move west across the mighty Mississippi River. With four wagons pulled by teams of horses and one yoke of cattle, several cows, two heifers, and other small animals, the young widow and his four children began the difficult journey. Taking his younger brother, Eli, and his sister, Elizabeth, the brave little group proceeded westward across the Illinois prairie. They carried the rose bush with them.

After making a successful passage across the Mississippi River, they traveled westward into Iowa. In the gentle, rolling hills of southern Iowa, George set down his claim. Before his cabin was built, he planted the rosebush and remembered how Frances had pruned it, fed it, and loved it.

The oldest son, Alonzo, became his father's farming partner. The younger brothers, John and James, were responsible for the care of their young sister, Saffa Jane, while Elizabeth transformed the barren cabin into a home. After the first winter the rose bush began to bud into soft pink blossoms and George was pleased. He told his children stories about their mother and the special way she tended the roses.

A few years later George married Elizabeth Stout and their family continued to grow.

When President Abraham Lincoln called for volunteers for the Union Army, both George and Alonzo answered the call. Both father and son saw battles at Shiloh, Paducah, Tuka, Tupilo, and Nashville. George died of fever in a Memphis hospital at the age of forty. He was buried in an unmarked grave and his name was later inscribed in a monument to Civil War veterans in Memphis, Tennessee.

Alonso became the man of the family when he returned home from the battlefields. He was pleased that the rose bush had continued to grow. Three years later, Alonzo married Lydia Ellen Goodwin and they became the parents of four daughters and two sons. The rose bush faithfully bloomed every spring.

One of the sons of Alonzo was my paternal grandfather, Clyde.

When George's second wife, Elizabeth, died, neighbors were appointed guardians of the two minor children. Through all the joys and hardships, births and deaths, the rose bush continued to bloom every spring.

After the death of Alonzo, his daughter Emma, moved the rose bush to her home until it was moved again to Centerville, Iowa, the home of her daughter Florence. Florence tended the rose bush until her daughter Betty Ann transplanted it at her home in Knoxville, Iowa.

The rose bush has been divided into three healthy bushes among family members—one is in Indiana, one in Missouri, and the third remains in Knoxville, Iowa. There, Betty Ann arranged for the third rose bush to be planted in a park near a museum where a plaque tells the story of the one hundred and sixty-five year old rose bush that has been lovingly tended and appreciated by five generations of our family.

Appendix 4

Revolutionary War Patriot

Thomas Cummings is my Revolutionary War patriot.

Born in Virginia in 1754, he served as a private in Capt. John Lewis' Company of the Second Virginia State Regiment commanded by Col. Gregory Smith during the Revolutionary War.

Thomas married Sarah Henry, a native of Virginia and a sister of Patrick Henry. They were the parents of five sons:

Uriah 1779-1831

William 1782-1847

Josiah 1796-1849

Eli 1799-1845

Joseph (dates unknown)

Thomas Cummings went to Perry County, Indiana, from Virginia by way of Washington County, Kentucky, where he bought land on Little Cane Creek about 1795. That same year, on September 26, he bought 208.3 acres of land in Tobin Township, between Rome and Derby, Indiana.

Northern Tobin Township saw much of the activities of Thomas Cummings and his sons. They were engaged in many of the early business enterprises of the county and were active in politics and in the development of their community. The son, Uriah, donated land for the public buildings when Rome was made the county seat.

Uriah's son, Isaiah, enlisted in the Army while on a flatboat trip to New Orleans and served in the Mexican War.

Thomas died in 1814 and Sarah died January 1, 1825. They were probably buried in a family graveyard which was washed away by Ohio River floods and all traces of it have disappeared from the family land.

And Thomas begat William;

William begat George;

George begat Alonzo;

Alonzo begat Clyde;

Clyde begat Carl

Carl is the father of James, Elaine, and Carolyn,

thus, making us the seventh generation of the family since the Revolutionary War.

This is the line of ancestry which was researched by my father's first cousin, Betty Ann Boden Crozier, making her eligible for membership in the patriotic service organization, **National Society of the Daughters of the American Revolution.**

With the privilege of using her national number, my research was much faster. In fact, it was my Dad who offered to write letters requesting the necessary records which I needed. Securing birth, marriage, and death certificates of three prior generations completed the research. I'm grateful to both of them. With this much research already done, the next generation of our family line will have a clear path of eligibility and acceptance into this elite organization.

.

I am very thankful to Betty for encouraging me to become a member.

My Mission Viejo (CA) Chapter of the National Society of the Daughters of the American Revolution in California includes knowledgeable people, hardworking, caring ladies, and some of the dearest friends a person could ever have.

Preserving history, helping to educate and honor young people with scholarships and awards, assisting our veterans, keeping patriotism alive, historical preservation, and researching our family histories are just some of our goals and purposes.

Appendix 5

Rev. Jesse Herbert

When the Bedford Methodist Church observed its sesquicentennial in November 2004, my brother James Cummings gave a portrayal of his great, great grandfather, Rev. Jesse Herbert. This ancestor was a circuit rider and a charter member of the Methodist Church in Bedford.

Here is Jim's script for that reenactment:

(Enters sanctuary carrying saddle bag over shoulder. Removes Bible from saddle bag, pauses, and begins)

"You can carry a Bible in a saddle bag, or you can carry a Bible in your hand. But I am convinced that the best place to carry a Bible is in your heart.

Good morning, my fellow Methodists and friends of the Methodist Church. My name is Rev. Jesse Herbert. My wife, Martha, and I moved from Iowa City to Bedford in 1854, the year this church was founded. Yes, Martha and I were two of the twenty-one charter members of the Bedford Methodist Church.

Please allow me to tell you a little about myself. I was born in Indiana in 1813, the fifth child of James and Barbara Herbert. I moved with my parents and brothers and sisters to Fulton County, Illinois, when I was a young man. Fulton County is just east of Keokuk, Iowa. There I met and married my dear wife, Martha Huffman. I was engaged in farming as my primary source of income during all of my working years, but in the early years of our marriage I became a pioneer Methodist minister, a circuit rider.

My first appointment was to a church in Knoxville, Illinois, in 1838. In September, 1839, I was the first Methodist minister appointed to a church in Richland, Iowa. In 1840 I was sent to Fairfield, Iowa, to start a Methodist church there. Two years later I began a series of moves that took me from Terra Haute, Indiana, to Cuba, Illinois, to Iowa City, Iowa, and finally to Bedford in 1854. My final assignment was to the Wray Memorial Methodist Church in Hopkins, Missouri, where I served from 1860 until I was called home to be with Jesus in 1873 at the age of fifty-nine years.

My last years were happy ones surrounded by family and friends. Martha and I lived southwest of Bedford just west of the Kurt Rowan place. The homestead is no longer there but it afforded a spectacular view of the 102 River Valley. Martha and I were laid to rest in the southeast corner of the Hopkins, Missouri, cemetery.

Patsey and I...that was Martha's pet name...I fondly referred to her as Patsey. Patsey and I had nine children and each and every one of them was dear and precious, but I would like to tell you about my oldest son, Norris, and my youngest son, Isaac.

Isaac was the seventh of our nine children. He was not quite twelve months old when we moved to Bedford in 1854. Isaac lived most of his life in the Bedford area where he was engaged in farming. He and his wife Matilda had three children. The middle child was a little girl, Florence...Florence Herbert, my granddaughter. In 1903 Florence married a young man from Davis County...he was from a little town around Bloomfield, Iowa. They moved back to Davis County and farmed for a time, and then he decided he wanted to become an auctioneer. Did I mention the young man's name? No, I did not. Excuse me. His name was Clyde Cummings. He attended the auctioneer school in

Trenton, Missouri, then Clyde and my granddaughter, Florence, and their son and daughter eventually wound up back in the Bedford area, where he developed a successful auction business. Their son was...perhaps some of you remember... Carl Herbert Cummings. He was my great grandson, and I understand that on two different occasions he served this church as an interim pastor. When we build a bridge we never know who might cross it. We never know who shall follow in our footsteps.

Our oldest son, Norris, was just a lad of fourteen when we moved to Bedford in 1854. Norris answered the call of patriotism. He left his young wife and baby and marched off to war with many other young men from this area. They just wanted to help President Lincoln hold the United States of America together. Norris was wounded in battle; shot through the leg. He was taken prisoner and wound up in that dreadful Confederate prison in Georgia called Andersonville. When Patsey and I got word from the War Department that Norris had been wounded and was being held prisoner in Andersonville...I can't describe how heartsick we were.

The Book of James in the New Testament, chapter 5, verse 15 tells us, "And the prayer of faith shall save the sick, and the Lord shall raise him up."

I think I prayed more at that period of my life than at any other. The conditions at Andersonville Prison were indescribable. Those poor young men lacked adequate food. They existed primarily on wormy corn meal. There was scarcely any shelter, water was in short supply, and medicine was non-existent. Men were dying by the score every day.

Then, as if Almighty God reached down and touched His hand to that hell on earth, a spring of cool pure water erupted from the ground...it continued to flow and made a stream of life-saving water right through the middle of Andersonville Prison. Hundreds, perhaps thousands of lives were saved by that miraculous blessing of pure water. Norris sat by the stream daily and bathed his wounded leg using his tin cup.

Now, there are two things that I know: Prayer is something we do on our time...answering prayer is something God does on His time. The other thing I know is this: Almighty God healed my son, and returned him safely to his family...and he lived to be an old man...eighty years old.

Please forgive me for rambling on about my family. I guess when you get to be 191 years old you're entitled to dote over your children a little bit.

The early church...that's what we're here to remember and celebrate today. Records indicate that pioneer Methodist missionaries came up from Missouri as early as 1843 and preached occasionally in the homes of the early settlers in this area. The first attempt to hold a public worship service was in the winter of 1849-1850 when there were fewer than forty people residing in what is now Taylor County, Iowa. Forty people...think of it...why, there are more than forty people sitting in this section of the sanctuary this morning. That was the total population of Taylor County, and yet they felt a need for public worship.

I was not the assigned pastor when our church was founded in 1854. Rev. J. M. Baker was the supply preacher of this circuit. Patsey and I were just members of a congregation that worshiped regularly though we didn't have a church building.

This magnificent old building and lovely sanctuary that we are worshiping in today was built in 1889 at a cost of about fourteen thousand dollars. It was the first of the four brick churches built in Bedford's early history: Methodist, Presbyterian, Baptist and Christian. I understand the Christian Church has since closed, the building removed and their congregation has united with the Presbyterian Church.

And I understand the Baptist folks just celebrated their 150 years last weekend. What a blessing! What a blessing for this community that so many have worshiped together for so long.

Oliver Wendell Holmes once said: "There is a little corner of my heart called reverence that needs to be nurtured once a week." He was correct. There is no real devotion without devotion. When we worship together people find strength. Those faithful in attendance bring a feeling of joy and encouragement to others and stability to the ongoing work of the congregation.

As I reflect on my life and experience as a soldier of Christ, I have learned the following: people are more important than things...and relationships are more important than accomplishments.

No matter who we are, where we are, or what our circumstances, each day is a blessing and a new beginning, and, with God's help, it's an opportunity to be better and to do better. Life never stands still; there is a constant change...today is GOOD, and tomorrow can be even better.

May God bless each and every one of you. This is my prayer for you today and tomorrow. Amen."

(Rev. Herbert places Bible in saddle bag, throws it over his shoulder and exits singing the chorus of *Blessed Assurance:* "This is my story, this is my song, praising my savior all the day long...")